CONSPIRED

CONSPIRED

RAMY ROMANY
with EMILY HACHE

NEW YORK

LONDON • NASHVILLE • MELBOURNE • VANCOUVER

Conspired

Published in New York, New York by Morgan James Publishing in partnership with Impact Publishing. Morgan James is trademark of Morgan James, LLC.
www.MorganJamesPublishing.com

The Morgan James Speakers Group can bring authors to your live event. For more information or to book an event visit The Morgan James Speakers Group at www.TheMorganJamesSpeakersGroup.com.

Cover photo courtesy of Prometheus Entertainment

ISBN 9781642791464 paperback
Library of Congress Control Number: 2018907235

Cover & Interior Design by:
Christopher Kirk
www.GFSstudio.com

In an effort to support local communities, raise awareness and funds, Morgan James Publishing donates a percentage of all book sales for the life of each book to Habitat for Humanity Peninsula and Greater Williamsburg.

Get involved today! Visit
www.MorganJamesBuilds.com

Table of Contents

THE EVIL ONE

Year 1907, The Valley of the Kings, Luxor, Egypt

Something was not right. Something was different, strange. The archeologist could feel it and so could his team of Egyptian excavators. They knew something was different from the moment they discovered the first limestone door.

The door lay buried below the tomb known as KV6, belonging to Rameses IX. Rameses IX was a pharaoh of the 20th Dynasty, and his tomb had been open to the world since antiquity. For hundreds of years, people visited Rameses IX's large, elaborately painted resting place. The archeologist knew that this limestone door, still sealed, must lead to a much older tomb. He felt a thrill run through him. Could he have discovered a tomb lost since antiquity? Could he be the archaeologist to finally open a tomb laden with treasure, untouched by thieves or raiders?

Something was not right. Once the archeologist made his way through the first door, he and his team found the remains of a second door. Someone had been here before. The archeologist was disappointed but still hopeful. Even though the tomb had been opened by someone in antiquity, it had been resealed by someone else. Maybe there were still treasures to find under the dust and rubble that clogged the entrance. The excavators worked diligently to open up the passageway. They uncovered twenty steps leading down into a small, dark chamber. As the explorer entered the tomb for the first time, being the first person to enter the tomb for maybe thousands of years, he realized that this tomb was unlike any he had seen before.

The walls were bare. He knew they should have been painted and full of inscriptions, instructions for the after life. When he looked up to the ceiling, he saw that some-how, over the years, water had seeped in. There was dust, debris, and chips had fallen from the ceiling all over the floor. Though he couldn't be sure at first, it looked like the tomb had been raided or flooded. Nevertheless, he descended down the twenty steps, through the main corri-dor and into the burial chamber. The air was heavy, and the smell of his gas lantern soon filled the room.

Something was not right.

The tomb was nearly empty. In the corridor lay the remains of a gilded shrine—an intricately carved panel and door, both rotting and badly damaged. In the burial cham-ber, objects were scattered around in a way that led the archeologist to believe that the tomb had been flooded—a piece of gilded furniture, four canopic jars (used in mum-mification to hold the vital organs of the deceased), a few damaged wooden boxes and faience objects, discolored and laying on the floor. Everywhere was the smell of must and rotten wood, and even though he wasn't a superstitious man, the explorer felt a chill—a sense of foreboding.

Along the southern wall of the main burial chamber, the archeologist found a rotted lion-head bier, and laying on this bier was a badly damaged coffin.

The Egyptian workers were on edge. It was bad luck to disturb the dead. At first the explorer couldn't put his finger on what made him uncomfortable. Was it because the tomb looked like it had been raided but with valuables left inside? Was it the bare walls? The rotting coffin with its lid slightly ajar?

He shook off the feeling. He was a man of science after all, an archeologist, and it was ridiculous to fear the dead. He examined the broken doors of the gilded shrine. Surely there would be some information about who had been buried in this tomb. The name of the king or the queen who was put to rest here would be revealed to him. He was shocked to find that the name of the person who built the shrine had been scratched out. It was the same with the canopic jars and the coffin. Everywhere there should have been a name, on every cartouche, the explorer found only scratch marks.

He turned to the coffin for more clues. It was unlike any he had seen in his career. It was shaped like a woman, and at first the archaeologist thought this must be a queen's mummy. But the face told a different story because it wore the long false beard of a king. A man. The most striking feature of the coffin was the face itself, or what was left of it. It had been hacked off. Whoever had buried this mummy wanted to wipe its identity from history.

In the Valley of the Kings, around the sarcophagi of the Pharaohs, the ancient priests would install several measures of protection. One of these were the so-called Cardinal Blocks, placed on each side of the sarcophagus according to the four cardinal directions, North, South, East, West. Ancient Egyptians believed that these blocks held magical powers, and each one was inscribed with a magic formula and hieroglyphic inscriptions written to protect the contents of the coffin from the evils of the outside world.

"It is I who hinder the sand from choking the secret chamber; I am for the protection of the deceased."

The Ancient Priests would place the stones facing out to be easily read by anyone who might disturb the dead. The stones were both a warning and a curse.

In the newly discovered tomb, the archeologist found four Cardinal Blocks. But there was a distinct difference, and, at first, the archeologist thought that there must be some mistake. The Cardinal Blocks of KV55 did not face out to protect the mummy from the outside world. Whoever had placed these bricks faced them in toward the coffin itself, as if, instead of protecting the mummy from the world, they were trying to protect the world from the mummy.

Whoever buried this mummy had trapped its spirit in its coffin, robbed it of eternal life, blotted out its name, erased its face and did everything in their religious power to obliterate and curse it.

Who was in this coffin? What had he or she done to arouse such hate and fear? One of the workers called to the archeologist from the corridor. He had found another clue.

Along the western wall, in the language of the ancient Egyptian High Priests, was a tiny inscription:

"The Evil One shall not live again."

Something was not right in KV55.

Chapter 1:

THE MAGNIFICENT

3200 Years Earlier, 1361 BC, Ancient Thebes, Egypt

Amenhotep III understood what it meant to be king. To lead a great empire like Egypt, a king had to be strong, sure, and openly powerful, but military strength and conquests were not enough. Leading through fear and intimidation was necessary at times, but to create a stable and prosperous society, a king also had to understand his people. The people needed to feel safe and have plenty to eat; they needed to believe in their pharaoh to do what was right and bring glory to the empire. Ruling by fear was never enough; an effective king commanded respect as well. Politics mattered. Diplomacy mattered. Listening to the people mattered.

Egypt's long history complicated matters further. For much of its early history, Egypt acted as two nations, Upper and Lower. Because the Nile runs from south to north, Upper Egypt was the southern half of the country, including the religious center of Thebes down into Nubia. Lower Egypt encompassed the Nile River Delta and major northern cities, Heliopolis (near modern-day Cairo) and

Memphis, which was the center of government. The rivalry between Upper and Lower Egypt always seethed under the surface, and if the king was perceived to be weak or the simmering resentments were allowed to boil over, Egypt would break in two. A divided Egypt was vulnerable to civil war and foreign occupation, as had happened two hundred years before the rule of Amenhotep when Hyksos invaders ruled over most of Lower Egypt. For an Egyptian pharaoh to be successful, he had to be a true sema-tawy, "The Uniter of the Two Lands".

As a uniter, Amenhotep knew he could not rule alone; he needed the support and consent of his court, his armies, his people, and especially in Egypt, the high priests. Pharaohs had always had a close but uneasy relationship with the various cults of Egypt's many gods. Religion and politics were inextricably linked to each other; both gods and kings could rise or fall based on the influence the high priests had on the pharaoh. Amenhotep learned from the generations before him the importance of keeping the peace among the different cults.

The most powerful of these cults, by far, was the cult of Amun. The god Amun, "The Hidden One", was the patron deity of Thebes. The god's cult rose to power almost three hundred years before Amenhotep became king. Amun was credited with aiding the Egyptian army in driving out occupying forces that ruled over Thebes for over a hundred years. As the cult of Amun amassed more wealth and power, they used their influence to install pharaohs that were sympathetic to their cult, and thus continued to amass even more wealth and power with each succeeding king.

Before long, the High Priests of Amun had enough power to challenge the divine authority of the pharaoh himself.

Their great temple at Karnak grew to become a city within the city, set in the heart of Egypt's major southern city and religious center, Thebes. The cult's infrastructure of priests, scribes and administrators influenced every aspect of Egyptian life, from their army of slaves, artisans, and merchants, to their vast agricultural estates to their shipping and mining concerns. Devotees of Amun inserted themselves in every branch of Egyptian government, from the military to the Pharaoh's court.

Dealing with the cult of Amun was like navigating a boat through dark, dangerous waters. Their high priests could not be dismissed or disrespected. At the same time, their power and wealth had to be contained. Pharaoh needed to harness their power for his own benefit but, somehow, not be overrun by it.

Amenhotep navigated these dark waters well. He managed to shut out much of Amun's devotees from high positions in his government, especially in the military. In exchange for their loss of political influence, he was generous with public displays of faith, allegiance, and money. His own birth name, Amenhotep, meant "Amun is pleased". In the temple of Karnak, he ordered massive construction projects, including pylons, colonnades, hundreds of statues, and new temples. These projects used tons of rich blue lapis lazuli, shining turquoise, and solid gold and silver. He conceived of and built one of Thebes's most remarkable sites, Luxor, as the birthplace of Amun himself. Luxor served two purposes. It both honored the cult of Amun and, at the same time, reaffirmed the Pharaoh's place as the living manifestation of Amun. Amenhotep managed the powerful cult by co-opting it for himself.

And so it was that Amenhotep III became known as a great builder and would eventually be called The Magnificent. He ruled over a golden age, wherein his people lived in peace, prosperity, and unprecedented growth.

Like all kings before him, Amenhotep's primary concern, apart from governing, was his future, specifically the succession of power at the time of his death. His legacy and his dynasty must live on in the ascension to the throne of his son. Even here, Amenhotep's plan seemed foolproof.

Amenhotep, like all royal Egyptians, married at a young age, but his marriage was unlike the royal unions of most of his predecessors. Amenhotep took the unprecedented step of marrying a commoner and then elevating her to the highest position in his harem, Great Royal Wife. Her name was Queen Tiye, and she would become one of the most beloved and revered figures in Egyptian history. Although her family were not of royal descent, they were wealthy, influential, and powerful. Her father, Yuya, who may not have been Egyptian at all but a foreigner, was a key advisor to Amenhotep one of his chief military officers. Queen Tiye's brother, Ay, was also a trusted adviser and high ranking military official who would go on to influence the court for many years. Her other brother, Aanen, was a high priest of Re in Thebes and another close ally to his brother-in-law, the king. Tiye herself was the most trusted confidant of all.

She was educated, beautiful and wise. Amenhotep was so attached to her that he once constructed a great lake for her in Malkata, and he built countless statues and monuments in her honor.

Amenhotep and his beautiful Great Royal Wife had many children but only two sons.

The eldest took after his parents in all of the best ways. They named him Thutmose, "True of Voice", and by all accounts he lived up to his name; he was both fair and wise. His father placed all of his trust in Prince Thutmose. As part of his plan to manage the religious cults of Egypt, Amenhotep named Prince Thutmose High Priest of Ptah in Memphis, thus ensuring the cooperation of Northern Egypt. He also appointed him Overseer of the Priests of Upper and Lower Egypt, joining the two regions. Ptah was the god of creation and thereby was the patron of many creative arts, like architecture, sculpture and shipbuilding. Amenhotep, through his son Prince Thutmose, demonstrated both his love of architecture and sculpture, but also his connection to the creator God of the northern city of Memphis.

With Queen Tiye at his side and Prince Thutmose in line to succeed him, Amenhotep could rest easy at night knowing that Egypt, today and for the foreseeable future, was in excellent hands.

There was little need to concern himself with his second son at all.

3200 Years Later, 1907 AD, Valley of the Kings, Luxor, Egypt

He found a name on the rotting door of the golden shrine.

The archeologist, Edward Ayrton, examined the damaged and forgotten relics in KV55, trying to discern what had happened here thousands of years ago. When he found the name, he could hardly believe his eyes.

Queen Tiye.

How could this be? How could this tomb—defiled, vandalized and cursed—how could this tomb belong to the beloved Queen Tiye? History had been so kind to her! Queen Tiye was one of Egypt's most famous and well-loved queens. She was the Great Royal Wife of Amenhotep The Magnificent, the Great Builder. Amenhotep was the greatest pharaoh of the 18th Dynasty and, perhaps, of all time.

At least some of the clues indicated that this sad tomb was Queen Tiye's final resting place. The coffin was shaped like a woman's, despite the presence of the false beard. The canopic jars, also, had a female shape. On closer examination, the damaged furniture seemed to belong to the Queen. Even the mummy itself, had the wider hips of a female.

What had Queen Tiye done to deserve such a fate? What part of her story had archeologists and historians missed that would transform a well-loved figure into one who was so despised?

Ayrton looked again at the coffin and the smashed, missing face. Had it once been the beautiful face of the Great Royal Wife of Amenhotep?

His eyes fell on the false beard. Surely there was another explanation.

Chapter 2:
THE OUTCAST

3200 Years Earlier, 1361 BC, 28th Regnal Year of Amenhotep

His birth name was Nepherkheperure, "Beautiful are the Manifestations of Re", and he was the second son of Amenhotep, The Magnificent. (For the purposes of this story, we will call him Nepher) No one knew much about him, except that he was an odd child, having little in common with his revered father and "fair, wise" brother, Prince Thutmose.

Perhaps his appearance set him apart. His face was long. His eyes bulged, and his lips were full. His arms and legs were thin and gangly, but his belly stuck out. He was not the perfect picture of virility and strength that the Egyptian people expected from their royal men.

In painting and sculpture, Ancient Egyptian artists idealized the royal family by giving them symmetrical features, high cheek bones, beautiful faces. The king himself was depicted as a living god with a perfect figure, strong arms and chest, and a powerful posture. Even though many of these paintings and sculptures exaggerated the perfection of the king, he, nevertheless, had to live up to this image as much as possible. His people expected him to rise to the defense of Egypt at a moment's notice and, even in times of peace, demonstrate his strength and agility through staged hunts or mock athletic displays. For Egyptians, strength and beauty were requirements in their king.

So it was no wonder that Amenhotep felt the need to keep his second son away from the prying eyes of his people. Nepher simply did not fit the bill of "living god."

Nepher was different from his father and brother in other ways. He was unusually bright, curious, passionate and held strong beliefs. As a young man he developed ideas that ran counter to much of his father's methods of governing. Nepher bristled at the way Amenhotep played politics with his court, with foreign kings from weaker nations, with his military officers, and especially with the High Priests of Egypt's various cults. Wasn't his father the king? Wasn't his father divine? Wasn't he the great pharaoh of a mighty empire and destined to join the gods to live forever after his death?

Nepher studied Egypt's history and dreamt of the days, long past, wherein the Pharaoh alone wielded power. He believed that the Pharaoh, as a living manifestation of the gods on earth, was the only person qualified to make important decisions. The young prince's father and grandfather were partly to blame for how Nepher developed his unorthodox views, but neither Amenhotep nor his father could have anticipated how far the odd young man would take them.

In an effort to loosen the grip that the religious cults had on the Egyptian people, especially the cult of Amun, Amenhotep and his father encouraged the rise of a new manifestation of the sun god. The sun's traditional manifestation in the North of Egypt was Re; Amun took on some of that role in the South, such that the high priests of Amun co-opted Re into their own cult, and the god became known as Amun-Re. This joining of the two gods did not sit well with all Egyptians, as the Northern and Southern Kingdoms were fierce rivals for almost all of their recorded history. Nevertheless, Amun-Re was the principal and most powerful god among all of the Egyptian pantheon.

During the reign of Amenhotep's father, a new manifestation of the sun god emerged. He was the Aten, the force behind both Amun and Re, the light and energy of the sun disc itself in its purest form. Aten was depicted as the orb of the sun with its rays reaching down like hands to bless the royal family, who were Aten's sole representatives on earth. Amenhotep and his father were clever in their use of this powerful god because the nature of the Aten asserted and confirmed the power of the king. The Aten didn't belong to the high priests; he belonged to the pharaoh.

There were ample political reasons why Amenhotep encouraged the rise of the Aten in Egyptian culture. As one of the most powerful civilizations on earth, Egypt had become home to many foreigners who brought their customs and their own faiths with them. Amenhotep's own father-in-law, Yuya, may have been foreign-born, and Amenhotep welcomed princesses from other kingdoms into his harem. Several of his most senior officials were of foreign descent, including Aper-el, his northern vizier. The Aten, as an all-powerful and unifying god, lessened the rivalry between Upper and Lower Egypt and also appealed to the growing international population. The sun, and by extension the Aten, was a universal symbol of divinity, a god whose light shone on everyone without prejudice all over the empire.

To young Nepher, the Aten represented the ultimate god, the highest god, bringing enlightenment (both literal and figurative) to the world and exclusive power to the king. If the other Egyptian gods were like the stars, then the Aten, by comparison, was the sun. The Aten did not require a complicated hierarchy of priests, secret rituals, or esoteric knowledge. The Aten was the light of the sun, illuminating all of nature with its divine rays. No wonder Nepher was so enchanted by it, and his parents did little to discourage their second son's religious zeal.

After all, what harm was there in allowing Nepher to indulge his beliefs? Amenhotep and Prince Thutmose, through their savvy political planning, had managed to placate all of the major religious cults. The Aten was an important religious and political tool, and there seemed to be no problem in allowing the second son of the pharaoh to wield it.

But Nepher's unconventional religious beliefs, coupled with his strange appearance, perceived weakness, high intelligence, and idealism made him something of a pariah at court. Amenhotep tried to soften his son's rough edges and keep him in check. When that proved too difficult, he sidelined Nepher and continued to focus his attention on preparing Prince Thutmose to ascend the throne.

What was life like for young Nepher—ugly, outcast, but at the same time intelligent and capable in his own way? He must have been frustrated by the endless political maneuvering and intrigue at court. He was probably jealous of the attention, the respect, and the honors lavished on his older brother. He must have known that everyone respected him to his face but whispered about him behind his back.

In his heart of hearts, Nepher believed that he was right about the Aten. The Aten was the god behind all of the other gods; he was the ultimate deity. Egypt and her great empire would eventually, someday, look to Aten (and only Aten) for its wealth, prosperity and blessings, and the pharaoh would be there as the sole representative of the great Aten's beneficence.

That day would come. Nepher was confident of that.

Amenhotep was approaching a milestone in his long reign, and preparations were under way for an event that would bring together the entire Egyptian Empire—the great Sed-festival commemorating Amenhotep's thirtieth year as pharaoh. Even though the event was over a year away, all of Thebes worked tirelessly to be ready.

The Sed-festival was more than a celebration of a ruler's long turn on the throne. It was a renewal of his divine right to reign, a rebirth of the kingship, and a confirmation of the union between the North (Lower Egypt) and the South (Upper Egypt). A king's first Sed-festival traditionally took place in the thirtieth year of his reign, with festivals every three years thereafter. There were religious ceremonies, visits from high ranking officials representing every corner of the Egyptian empire, lavish reenactments of key myths, and ritual tests of the pharaoh's strength and skill.

The most famous of these tests was a race with the Apis bull. The king ran the entire course twice—once for Upper and once for Lower Egypt. Each run consisted of four "laps" from end to end of the course, with each end representing the connection between the north and south. By completing the course, the king proved that he was still capable of uniting the empire. He was coronated again with the two crowns of Egypt—the Red Crown for Lower and the White Crown for Upper Egypt.

After proving himself on the race course, the king reenacted a key story from Egyptian myth. Osiris, the sun god, was betrayed and murdered by his brother Set. Set put Osiris's body in a coffin and threw it into the Nile, but the god of the Nile delivered the coffin to the sea where it washed up on the shore of Syria and settled in the trunk of a tree. The king of Syria, intrigued by the rapid growth of the tree and unaware of the god inside it, ordered the tree to be cut down and made into a pillar for his palace. Soon, Osiris's wife, Isis, who had been searching the world for Osiris's body, discovered the coffin inside the pillar. She retrieved Osiris's body and was able to bring him back to life. The tree became known as the Pillar of Djed, and each pharaoh raised a version of this pillar as part of their

Sed-Festival. It was a powerful symbol of renewal and Osiris's defeat of death.

Amenhotep planned to take this ritual one step further and stage a large boat procession. The pharaoh, along with the statues of various deities, would sail in barges to recreate the voyage of Osiris through the underworld. It would be a grand renewal of Amenhotep's reign, a reassertion of his power, and an opportunity for his heir, Crown Prince Thutmose, to present himself to the empire by serving in various important ritual capacities.

In the excitement of the preparations, no one could have expected that the Crown Prince would not live to see the festival at all.

Chapter 3:

THE HEIR

The death of Crown Prince Thutmose could not have happened at a worse time. Economically and politically, Egypt was both powerful and stable. Her army was strong; her enemies feared and respected her, and her allies welcomed her protection and willingly pledged their loyalty to the pharaoh. But Amenhotep was over forty years old and had been pharaoh for almost three decades. While some Egyptians lived well into their sixties, forty was by no means young. The Sed-festival that Amenhotep was so busy planning wasn't just a way for him to prove his continued strength and capacity to lead. It was also a chance to demonstrate that his heir, Crown Prince Thutmose, was ready to take the throne.

By all accounts, Prince Thutmose was ready. By naming him "Overseer of the Priests of Upper and Lower Egypt" and "High Priest of Ptah in Memphis", his father had trusted him with some of the highest religious, and by extension political, stations in the land and had specifically named Thutmose his heir. His death was a devastating blow to the royal family and to Egypt itself.

No one knows what happened to Prince Thutmose. In the historical record, he is there one minute and gone the next, almost as if he never existed. For a prince who was so influential, loved, trusted, and revered, what could have happened to him? How could he have just disappeared? Why did Amenhotep's court suddenly stop mentioning him altogether?

An "ordinary death" by accidental or natural causes would not have caused Prince Thutmose to be wiped from the historical record. Other prominent figures in Egyptian history died of natural causes, and there was no need to hide what had happened to them. Women died in childbirth, plagues and natural disasters took both the high and low born. But what was unforgivable, especially for the son of the pharaoh, was defeat.

Nothing was more important than strength: winning wars, conquering lands, stability, wisdom, victory. The weaknesses of government—defeat in battle, betrayal, treachery, failure—were never recorded. The ancient Egyptians believed in everlasting life, so much so that pharaohs carried their most prized possessions with them into their tombs, including food, drink, clothing, even horses, chariots and weapons. Only what they took with them lived on. This belief extended to their history; only the history they recorded lived on. If the Egyptians failed to record a defeat or failure or coup, then it never happened. The event was wiped from both history and eternity at the same time.

The pharaoh himself rarely ventured into battle unless there was an existential threat to the empire, but sons of the pharaoh, especially those who hoped one day to become pharaoh themselves, would often join the Egyptian army to prove their strength, their worth, and their ability to lead.

Prince Thutmose may have died trying to prove himself to be worthy of his father's crown. His death would have been viewed as a weakness and a disgrace, a sign that he was never fit for the throne in the first place.

But there is another possible answer to what happened to Crown Prince Thutmose, and the key may lie in the Old Testament of the Bible.

The Exodus of the Jews out of Egypt is one of the biggest events recorded in the Old Testament. The Bible claims that the Egyptian army, along with the pharaoh, were all killed by drowning in the Red Sea after Moses called on God to part the waters to allow the Jews to flee from Egypt to freedom and safety. Of course, the Egyptians recorded no such event.

Most historians agree that if the Exodus happened at all, it would have taken place during the 18th or 19th Dynasties in Egypt. Historians also agree that the actual pharaoh, in a time of peace and prosperity, would never lead a war in person against a slave rebellion. Pharaoh would not risk his life in this way, but he may have been willing to risk the life of his son.

Amenhotep, eager to show his son's strength and fitness for the throne, may have sent his eldest son, Prince Thutmose, on an expedition to return the enslaved Jewish people to Egypt. It is exactly the kind of mission that would appear daring and brave but not actually be too risky.

If Amenhotep sent his son on such a mission, it was a grave miscalculation. Something went wrong. Prince Thutmose, "True of Voice," fair and wise, never came home. He would never be king of Egypt. Amenhotep's grand, full-proof plan of succession had failed.

Surely, Amenhotep and Queen Tiye bitterly mourned the loss of their son, on whom they had put all of their hopes and dreams for the future of their dynasty. Just when they were preparing for a great celebration of the pharaoh's wisdom and power, they had to face the death of their child. They also had to cover up the devastating and humiliating defeat.

To make matters worse, Amenhotep needed a new heir. He could not—he would not—let the 18th Dynasty end with him. He knew that if he didn't come up with a suitable heir, and soon, the political vultures of the court would find one for him. With all of his careful planning shattered in an instant, Amenhotep turned to his second son, Nepher, the outcast, the odd one, the pious and passionate follower of the Aten.

Nepher would have to do.

Chapter 4:

A SHARED TOMB

When Edward Ayrton, the fifty-nine year old British Egyptologist, discovered KV55, he had already been working in the Valley of the Kings for several years. Like most archeologists in the early 1900's, Ayrton was primarily interested in hitting the mother lode—an undisturbed, intact tomb, filled with gold and treasures. Ayrton's sponsor, Theodore Montgomery Davis, an American attorney and treasure-hunter, bankrolled exploration in the King's Valley beginning in 1902. Davis's interest in the King's Valley was treasure, and he passed this mission on to the archeologists he hired to supervise his digs.

When Ayrton discovered and opened KV55, he was probably more disappointed than intrigued. He certainly never expected that this discovery would turn out to be one of the most controversial tombs ever uncovered. Even Ayrton's own team could not agree on who might be buried there. There were several theories, all hotly debated.

The most obvious choice was, of course, Queen Tiye, and there was compelling evidence to support the mummy being the Great Royal Wife of Amenhotep. The golden shrine belonged to Queen Tiye as did several of the furniture fragments. And the coffin, despite its false beard, clearly had been made for a woman. The hair, the shape of the body, and the inscription at the bottom all pointed to it being originally intended for a woman...and a royal woman at that.

The false beard was the main problem with this theory. Why would the ancients add a false beard to the coffin of a woman? There were a few possible explanations.

The first was that the coffin originally was made for a woman, but, for some mysterious reason, was later co-opted for a man, specifically a pharaoh. There was evidence to support this idea beyond the false beard. The arms on the outside of the coffin were crossed as if they were holding the crook and flail, the two royal scepters of Egypt. The coffin had been retrofitted in antiquity with a uraeus, one of the two crowns worn by the king of Egypt. The uraeus, or cobra, was the age-old symbol for the goddess Wadjet, the protectress of Northern Egypt. The uraeus, along with the white vulture, the symbol of Nekhbet (the protector goddess of Southern Egypt), were symbols used by the pharaoh and only the pharaoh. All of these pieces of evidence formed the argument that the mummy was indeed a man, and a king, who had "borrowed" the coffin of one of his royal wives.

The second theory was that somehow this coffin held an as-yet-unidentified lady. However, for this theory to work, this lady, whoever she was, must have at some point held the rank of King.

It was rare but not completely unheard of for a woman to be King of Egypt. By the time Ayrton was excavating in the Valley of the Kings, archeologists and historians knew that at least one of Egypt's kings was a woman. Her name was Hatshepsut, and she reigned during the first half of the 18th Dynasty—the same dynasty that tomb KV55 and this mummy seemed to come from.

Even though she was a woman, Hatshepsut wasn't called "Queen" because that title belonged only to the wife (or wives) of the king. The ruler of Egypt was always masculine. When Hatshepsut ascended to the throne of Egypt, her gender changed for political purposes, from female to male. Scribes described her deeds using male pronouns; they called her King, and all of her paintings and statues depicted her with the false beard of the pharoah. The beard symbolized power and wisdom, and by wearing one, Hatshepsut showed her people that she was equal to a male king in every respect, just as powerful, just as wise.

Hatshepsut was the only "female King" known to have existed, but it was possible, in theory at least, that there were others. The coffin in KV55 might hold another woman who had somehow risen to the highest office of Pharaoh.

Ayrton knew this much for sure: if the mummy was indeed a woman pharaoh, she couldn't be Queen Tiye. Queen Tiye had always been identified as the Great Royal Wife; there was no indication whatsoever that she had ever ascended to the most powerful position in Egypt. Queen Tiye was influential, respected, and held a large share of the responsibility of governing Egypt, but she was never a King. Even if she had, at some point, become a co-regent, she would still be identified as the wife of her husband.

Ayrton brought two doctors to Egypt to determine the gender of the mummy who rested in the strange male-female coffin. The doctors noted that the mummy's arms were positioned in a way that was traditionally associated with a woman; the pelvic bones were heavily damaged but appeared to be feminine, and the mummy seemed to lack male genitalia. Because of this examination, Ayrton and Davis were convinced that the mummy was a woman. Theodore Davis, a world renowned archaeologist, published a paper announcing the discovery as The Tomb of Queen Tiye.

He spoke too soon, because only a few months later, an anatomist named Grafton Elliot Smith identified the mummy as a man of around twenty five years old.

Everywhere Ayrton turned the mystery grew. Searching for more clues, he examined the canopic jars found near the coffin. And again, things were not adding up.

Canopic jars come in a set of four, in every tomb and with every burial. They hold the internal organs of the mummy—the stomach, the intestines, the liver and the lungs. These organs were removed as part of the mummification process. The four jars were associated, like much of Egyptian ritual, with the cardinal directions, North, South, East, and West and also various animals. The jar for the North contained the lungs. Its lid was carved in the shape of a baboon's head. A Jackal-headed jar contained the stomach and represented East. West was a falcon and held the intestines. Finally, the South was lidded with a human head, usually a carved in the image of the deceased. It contained the liver.

This last jar presented another intriguing mystery for Ayrton. The human head on the jar in KV55 was a woman, but she bore no resemblance to any of the known depictions of Queen Tiye. This mystery woman was too young, and her wig and jewelry were completely different from what was known to be worn by the Great Royal Wife.

Ayrton found one of the only intact cartouches in the tomb on one of the jars. These jars belonged to Kiya. Kiya, Ayrton knew, was a lesser wife of Nepher. Little was known about her, except that at some point around the tenth year of Nepher's reign, Kiya disappeared.

Ayrton hoped that solving the mystery of the canopic jars would shed light on who exactly was laid to rest in that coffin. Now, it seemed, he was faced with an even more confounding possibility; this tomb may have been the final resting place of not just one, but as many as three, members of the royal family.

During mummification, the only major organ left in the body was the heart. Ancient Egyptians believed that the deceased needed their hearts for the trials of the afterlife.

In the Egyptian underworld of Duat, the dead underwent various tests to prove their worth and secure their place in the afterlife. The most famous of these trials was the Weighing of the Heart. The Egyptians believed that the actions one took during life had an effect on the heart in the afterlife. If a person had lived in maat, loosely translated as "truth" or "righteousness", then their heart would reflect their goodness. In the Weighing of the Heart test, the dead placed their heart on a scale against a feather. If the heart proved lighter than the feather, they had lived in maat and were welcomed into the afterlife.

Ayrton must have wondered about the mystery mummy who had been laid to rest here and the others who may have shared this small, desolate tomb. Would the Evil One's heart have passed the test, or would he (or she) be found unworthy of everlasting life?

Chapter 5:

THE NEXT AMENHOTEP

1358 BC, 31st Regnal Year of Amenhotep III's Reign, Thebes

With the death of his eldest son and heir, Amenhotep the Magnificent's reign suffered a devastating blow. The next eight years would see his enthusiasm for his role decline. It was a sad fall for a man who began his reign as a bright and energetic young pharaoh who built such wonders for his people. He was still a relatively young man, well under fifty years old, but he had grown lazy and fat and lost interest in just about everything but his large harem. Even in the last two or three years of his reign, he continued to add wives to his household. He took to wearing long, flowing robes and lounging around his sprawling palace at Malqata. His health took a turn for the worse; his decaying teeth hurt, and he lacked the energy to fulfill his duties.

Amenhotep's decline was surely linked to the death of Prince Thutmose. The loss of his favorite son combined with the stress of preparing his second son for the throne took its toll on the aging pharaoh.

In the 18th Dynasty, succession was not just a matter of turning the reins of power to the eldest living son. The eldest male child of the pharaoh was usually the first choice to inherent the throne, but he was by no means guaranteed the position. Heirs could, and often were, challenged by their younger brothers, their uncles, and even in some cases outsiders. If the pharaoh wanted his eldest son to succeed him, he had to line up the approval of the wealthy and influential upper classes, the court, the military, and the high priests of the religious cults scattered throughout the empire. The king had to convince his people that his son was the best choice to carry Egypt into the future.

Amenhotep had invested years in building support for Prince Thutmose. Now, he had to rally support again, this time for a less desirable candidate, his second son Nepher.

At any other time in history, Nepher would have had no chance to become pharaoh. There was something to disqualify him with every major faction in the upper echelons of society. His perceived weakness damaged him with the military; his unusual beliefs were anathema to the high priests; his appearance and strong personality made him unpopular at court. He was lucky, indeed, that Amenhotep was his father and Queen Tiye was his mother. His parents were his only saving grace.

Amenhotep was an excellent politician, and he knew how to use propaganda to get things done. Queen Tiye, who was respected and loved at court, was no doubt motivated to exploit every possible advantage for her second son to become pharaoh. There were probably other sons, born to lesser wives, who threatened Nepher's claim to the throne. If these lesser sons succeeded, Queen Tiye and her family would be shut out of the royal household. Nepher had to become king.

The first step the King and Queen took was to change Nepher's name. Ancient Pharaohs' names were not necessarily the names given at birth. Royalty often changed their names, or had several names that they were known by. A king could have as many as five names, including a birth name, a coronation name, and a god name. Most ancient Egyptian kings are known by their coronation names, all of which include the name of a god.

For example, Amenhotep means, "The God Amun is satisfied." Ramses means, "The Son of God Ra". Some kings chose their names because of their beliefs and their spiritual connection to a specific god. But if there was a question about the fitness of a king, then a good way to ease fears and gain support was to choose a name that would be popular. And there was no Egyptian god more popular than Amun. The Egyptian people trusted and respected Amenhotep, so it was also reasonable to want to connect Nepher more closely to his strong father by linking their names. King Amenhotep wanted the Egyptians to believe that Nepher would be just as powerful, just as wise, and just as successful a leader. He wanted them to believe that his awkward, unusual son would follow in his footsteps and that Egypt would be as prosperous under Nepher as it was under Amenhotep. So he changed Nepher's name to Amenhotep IV.

It's possible that Amenhotep also made Nepher his co-regent, but this is murkier in the historical record. If he elevated Nepher to rule alongside him in the last years of his reign, it would have sent a powerful signal that Nepher could be trusted as the heir. Co-regencies, wherein a king appointed his successor to rule alongside him for a transition period, were common in ancient Egypt. In fact, co-regencies were more common than traditional successions, where the heir inherits the throne only when the king dies. Co-regencies served several purposes. They provided continuity of government and a smooth transition from one administration to the next. They allowed the people and the systems of government to adjust to new leadership, and they solidified the position of the heir not just as "next in line" but as an actual ruler, with all of the titles and responsibilities of his predecessor. Once a pharaoh selected a co-regent, it was almost impossible to take that title away.

One thing is certain, Amenhotep the father stepped out of the limelight during the last years of his reign, and this opened a power vacuum that the High Priests of Amun sought to fill. For the previous several generations, the cult of Amun and the pharoah's family had achieved an uneasy balance of power, with the pharaoh honoring the cult publicly while actively keeping it in check privately. But with Amenhotep senior weakened and with a controversial heir, the Amun priests saw an opportunity to shift the balance in their favor.

So began a tug of war between the High Priests of Amun and the royal household that would continue for the next three decades. Whether Amenhotep delegated his power to Nepher as co-regent or to the still vibrant and savvy Queen Tiye is unclear. Perhaps both mother and son took up the slack left by Amenhotep. Queen Tiye was well aware of the stakes of doing nothing. She knew that, both for her own personal power and for the stability of Egypt, the Amun priests must not be allowed to take control of the country. If her husband was no longer willing to provide strong leadership, she would, and she would teach her son, Nepher, how to work with the Amun cult, or around them if necessary. For the last eight years of her husband's reign, Queen Tiye was a driving force in holding Egypt together.

Nepher bristled at these machinations. They were exactly the kind of political maneuvering that he found unnecessary and tiresome, but even Nepher recognized that challenging his parents' choices would only lead to disaster for himself and his prospects. If Nepher ever wanted to become pharaoh and usher in a new age of enlightenment and a return to the glory of the pharaohs of old, he had to tolerate his parents' politics for the time being.

So Nepher bided his time. He changed his name. He supported his father in the sed-festivals for his 34th and 37th regnal years; he toned down his own ideology and his religion. He "went along to get along," as they say. And he prepared for the day in the not too distant future when his father would join the gods in the afterlife. Then, Nepher would call the shots.

Chapter 6:

YEAR ONE

1351 BC, 1st Regnal Year of Nepher's Reign, Thebes

"The falcon is flown to heaven, and Amenhotep IV has arisen in his place." So came the announcement that Amenhotep III was dead and Nepher (now called Amenhotep IV) was Egypt's new king.

There was no ritual more sacred, complex, or important than the funeral rites of a pharaoh. The process took months. No expense was spared. The Egyptians believed that the pharaoh was transitioning from life to the afterlife, where he would transform into a divine being and take his place among the immortal gods. If the priests and the pharaoh's family failed to perform the funeral rites properly, he would be condemned to oblivion. He would fail the tests set for him by the gods; he would lack everything he needed to thrive in the afterlife.

The mummification of the pharaoh's body took over seventy days. During this time, the body was washed in wine and exotic spices, and the major internal organs, except the heart, were removed and preserved in the canopic jars. The Egyptians believed that the brain was not an important organ; knowledge and thought came from the heart, so the brain was extracted by inserting a hook up through the nose and drawing it out. It was not preserved. The body was then packed in natron, a mineral salt common to Egypt. Over the next two months, the natron drew all of the moisture from the body, completely drying and preserving it. Finally, the desiccated body was removed from the natron, washed in more wine and spices, and wrapped in fine strips of linen. Hidden within the strips of linen were precious amulets and totems to protect the pharaoh in the afterlife.

After mummification, the body was placed in a set of three elaborate nesting coffins, fashioned to resemble the dead king. The innermost coffin was the most magnificent, made from solid gold. The outer coffins were works of art in themselves—intricately carved wood, covered in gold leaf, and encrusted with lapis, turquoise and other precious stones.

The preparation of the tomb was equally extensive and lavish. Amenhotep began construction on his tomb during the early days of his reign. For the Egyptians, their eternal homes were more important to them and more carefully constructed than the ones they built for their day-to-day living. Palaces and houses of ancient Egypt were not built to last. Constructed from simple mud bricks, they could be raised and torn down quickly and easily. As a result, very little of these structures have survived into the modern era. Ordinary houses and palaces were not built to survive the ravages of time.

Tombs were. Carved into solid limestone, these vast man-made caves were built to last for thousands of years, because the occupants needed these structures for eternity. Tombs were painted with lush scenes of the afterlife among the gods. Painstaking instructions were carved into the walls to guide the deceased as they navigated their way through the underworld. Room after room after room provided the king plenty of space to spread out, and additional rooms were set aside for his wife and children when the time came for them to join him.

The construction on Amenhotep's tomb began at the beginning of his reign, but tombs were rarely finished before the death of their owner. So there was a flurry of activity in the seventy days between the king's death and his final laying to rest. Painters, plasterers and carvers rushed to put the finishing touches on the interior of the tomb. They added last minute information, recorded final important historical moments, and wrote the last instructions the king would need for the afterlife.

Nepher, as the pharaoh's successor, and the royal family had important roles to play in sending Amenhotep off to eternity. Nepher led a massive funeral procession, which included his father's wives and children, the viziers of both Upper and Lower Egypt, and a large group of dignitaries and nobles from all over the empire. Professional mourners, dancers, and musicians were employed to send the great king on his final journey. And of course, all of the High Priests of the various cults were present. The procession included the coffin, carried on an ornate sledge drawn by oxen, followed by another to carry the canopic jars, and then, of course, the funerary items—the chariots, furniture, personal objects, and food and wine that Amenhotep would want in the afterlife.

The funeral procession wound its way through Thebes and into the desert to the Valley of the Kings. Once there, Nepher performed the Opening of the Mouth Ceremony for his father. This most sacred ceremony was believed to reawaken the dead. Priests stood Amenhotep's coffin upright, and Nepher touched the body with a magical staff made especially for the ritual. In this way, the five senses— sight, hearing, taste, touch and smell—were restored to the deceased. The Opening of the Mouth was important as a religious ritual because it brought Amenhotep back to life in the underworld, but it benefitted Nepher, too. As a sacred public display, it solidified Nepher's position as heir to the throne. Once Nepher brought his father "back to life", the coffin was carried into the tomb and laid to rest in a massive, granite sarcophagus. All of the funerary objects were arranged in the tomb for the pharaoh's use in the afterlife, and the tomb was sealed...forever.

With his father safely dispatched to the heavens, Nepher officially began his reign.

Nepher was about twenty years old when he became the sole ruler of Egypt. Even though he may have spent several years as co-regent with his father, he had never ruled independently. Now was his chance to make his mark, to set himself and his reign apart from that of his larger-than-life father.

Amenhotep was a tough act to follow. He had been a great politician, a prolific builder, and a strong leader. His allies trusted and respected him, and his diplomatic skills had ushered in an unprecedented period of peace and prosperity. His construction projects were some of the most extensive and magnificent that Egypt had ever seen. And even though Egypt had not been involved in any serious military conflicts during Amenhotep's reign, the old pharaoh valued his vast armies and made sure that the enemies of Egypt would think twice before they attacked her or her allies.

Nepher was also eager to demonstrate Egypt's greatness, but he had a different point of view on what was important and where resources should be spent. One thing was clear: Nepher wanted to follow in his father's footsteps first and foremost by being a great builder. Maybe it was because he watched, as a youth, the incredible projects commissioned by his father at Karnak and Luxor. Maybe he wanted to see his own image and that of his family in statues and temples all over Thebes. Perhaps he wanted to elevate his favored god, the Aten, by making him more visible against his rival, Amun. Whatever the reason, Nepher took an instant and passionate interest in the construction of public buildings and temples.

At first glance, this work could not have been more ordinary and consistent with what Amenhotep had built. Nepher completed Amenhotep's unfinished temple at Soleb, where he depicted himself worshipping the deified version of his father. At Karnak, Nepher finished the decoration of the pylons his father had begun. He chose conventional images carved and painted in the traditional style: Nepher making offerings to the gods, Nepher smiting the heads of foreign enemies.

The only hint that great change was coming was in the

subtle shift of focus to the god Re-Horakhti. Re-Horakhti was the version of the sun god most associated with the dawn, the bright disc of the sun rising in the east. He was depicted as a falcon-headed man who wears a sun disc on his head. Nepher depicted himself making offerings to this version of the sun god on the southern pylon at Karnak and hinted further at the direction he was headed with Re-Horakhti: "he who rejoices in the horizon in his name,'Sunlight that is in the Disc.'"

At court, there was little real change at first, and it seemed that Egypt would continue in much the same way it had under Amenhotep, much to the relief of the military, the high priests, and the wealthy and influential nobles. The royal family continued to live in Thebes at the Malqata palace. Queen Tiye, now the King's mother, continued to advise her son and wield her vast political influence. Her brother, Ay, stayed on as royal adviser. And even though Nepher began changing the religious focus from Amun to Re-Horakhti, the cult of Amun was allowed to continue its work, unrestricted. Money still flowed into the cult's coffers; additions were made to Karnak and Luxor; Nepher kept his father's name, Amenhotep. For the first few years of Nepher's reign, the Amun priests breathed a sigh of relief. Perhaps their concerns about the new king and the changes he might bring were unfounded.

Not all was business as usual, however. With Nepher's ascension to the throne, new faces came onto the scene, and their influence on the young pharaoh would have lasting consequences. The most powerful of these new players was also the most beautiful. Her name was Nefertiti.

Chapter 7:

THE WIFE

3200 Years Later, 1912 AD, The Ruins of Amarna, Egypt

They were lucky to have found it at all. Ludwig Borchardt, an archeologist with the German Oriental Society, had been working in the ruins of Amarna for five years. He and his team had surveyed most of the city and were digging exploratory trenches along the "High Priest Street" in the eastern section. When they reached the southern end of Amarna, they stumbled upon the studio, buried beneath thousands of years of desert sand. The ancient studio belonged to the royal sculptor Thut, the "Chief of Works," and it soon became clear to Borchardt and his men that Thut was no ordinary sculptor.

At first, the find yielded little. Thut, like most of the residents of ancient Amarna, had abandoned the city to return to Thebes. He and his assistants had taken everything of value with them. What they left behind were "worthless" plaster casts of heads and faces of unidentified noble subjects, disembodied arms and legs that would never find their way onto their intended statues, unfinished sculptures of individuals who, for whatever reason, were deemed not worth saving. Thut had piled these miscellaneous items, over fifty of them, into a small storeroom, perhaps with the intention of someday returning to retrieve them. He never did.

Thousands of years later in 1912, this jumble of cast-offs held a different meaning and much more value. Among the plaster casts and random limestone arms and legs, Borchardt stumbled onto one of the greatest finds of ancient Egyptian sculpture. It would become as iconic as King Tut-ankhamen's golden death mask and just as famous.

This treasure had originally been stored on a shelf, but sometime in the three thousand years of subsequent neglect, the shelf deteriorated, and the bust crashed to the floor. Years of dust, decay and debris covered it, so that when Borchardt's workman found it, it was completely buried. When he pulled the bust from the rubble, Borchardt knew instantly that he had found something unique, remarkable and priceless.

It was the limestone bust of a woman of high position, wearing an unusual blue crown. The crown excited Borchardt, who recognized it immediately. It was tall, cylindrical and adorned with golden ribbons and the distinctive uraeus, or cobra, associated with Lower Egypt. Around the woman's neck was an extravagant painted collar that, in real life, would have been made of lapis, turquoise and gold. The shape of the bust resembled that of a flower, with the woman's long neck as the stem, and the enigmatic face and high crown as the flower itself. She was incredibly beautiful with a swan-like neck, high cheekbones, large black-rimmed eyes, red lips and perfectly symmetrical features.

Her chin was lifted, her expression peaceful and haughty. She was magnificent.

There was only one ancient Egyptian woman who was commonly depicted wearing such a crown, and it just so happened that she lived in Amarna at the same time that Thut created this sculpture.

This was Nefertiti, the Great Royal Wife, Mistress of Upper and Lower Egypt. And if the striking sculpture Borchardt had found was any indication, she lived up to her name which meant "The Beautiful One Has Arrived."

𓆣 𓏤 𓄿 𓀀 𓏭

1351 BC, 1st Regnal Year of Nepher's Reign, Thebes

Nepher had many wives, both Egyptian and foreign. The kings of Egypt's allies and vassals often sent their daughters to Egypt's royal court as both a way to increase their influence on the pharaoh and to insure a strong, personal connection that led to economic and military support from Thebes. The children born from these marriages wielded power and influence, and if a wife bore a son, both mother and child had the chance to be elevated to Great Royal Wife and Crown Prince.

Nefertiti and Nepher were married at the beginning of his reign. Nefertiti was likely a teenager at the time. Who she was, where she came from, and who her parents were are all unclear. She may have been from the south—a Nubian princess or from as far away as Ethiopia. Her fashion sense indicated an affinity for southern Egyptian style; she was famous for wearing wigs that closely resembled the curly, bobbed hairstyles of male Nubian warriors. Her devotion to Nepher's new brand of monotheism has led to speculation that Nefertiti may have been Jewish, or a believer in a religion that would evolve into Judaism. Judaism originated at about this time in history, and it is entirely possible, if Nefertiti did hail from Nubia or Ethiopia, that she could have come from the early Jewish communities there.

Another likely origin is that she was the daughter of the royal advisor, Ay, who also happened to be Nepher's uncle. This would have made Nefertiti and Nepher cousins and Nefertiti a niece to the vibrant and powerful Queen Tiye. As a child, Nefertiti was cared for by Ay's wife, Tey. Tey was never identified as Nefertiti's mother, so Nefertiti may have been a daughter of an unknown first wife, whose name has been lost to history.

Whatever Nefertiti's origins, her power over the young pharaoh was clear. Nepher loved her deeply and honored her above all of his other wives. From the very beginning of Nepher's reign, Nefertiti held an unprecedented position of power. She accompanied Nepher everywhere; she participated in religious rituals and ceremonies of state that were usually reserved for men. On temple walls, she was shown making offerings to the gods and smiting female enemies. Both of these activities were usually reserved for the pharaoh alone. Nepher made her his partner in everything.

She was committed to Nepher's religious reforms. She enthusiastically endorsed the rise of the Aten as Egypt's premiere deity. Whether this belief was to ingratiate herself with her husband or because she was an honest and devout believer herself, Nepher granted her unprecedented power in the new religion. With Nefertiti, Nepher created something of a religious trinity with the Aten as the heavenly creator, Nepher as its only son, and Nefertiti as a mother goddess and partner in serving the Aten on earth.

There were other wives and consorts, and Nefertiti knew that each of these women were a potential threat to her position and power. Some were foreign-born princesses from allies and vassal states like Mittani, Enisasi, and Babylon. Some were holdovers from Amenhotep's reign. Nepher "inherited" his father's harem when the old king passed away. Even Nepher's sisters would have been potential rivals to Nefertiti. Incest was taboo among the lower classes of Egypt, but it was common and even encouraged in the royal family. Pharaoh's incestuous relationships with his sisters, cousins, and even in some cases, his own daughters was just another way to preserve the royal blood lines. All of these women, and they were many, would have posed a threat. That threat would double if any of them bore the king a son.

One rival in particular was especially troubling to Nefertiti. Her name was Kiya. Kiya and Nefertiti were a study in contrasts. Nefertiti was aloof, dignified, and regal. Kiya was pretty and cute in a more accessible way. Her name means "monkey," and it's easy to imagine her bringing a charming mischievousness and fun to the weightiness of royal life. Nepher was almost as fond of Kiya as he was of Nefertiti. He memorialized her in statues and carvings, and he bestowed on her the honorific, "Greatly beloved wife of the king of Upper and Lower Egypt." She did not have the status of the "Great Royal Wife," but she was dangerously close. If Kiya were to bear Nepher a son, Nefertiti's place at court would be tenuous at best.

If Nefertiti's father was Ay and her aunt was Queen Tiye, she had powerful allies in the palace. Her father and aunt would do everything in their power to keep Nefertiti on the throne. They would never let some upstart "Monkey" replace their own flesh and blood. Even if Kiya managed to give Nepher a son, they would find a way to hold onto their family's hard-won power. Of course, if Nefertiti had a son of her own, there would be nothing to fear from any other woman.

So, Nefertiti set to work on her most important duty as the Great Royal Wife, the bearing of the king's children. As Nepher entered the second year of his reign, Nefertiti welcomed their first child. If Nefertiti was disappointed that their first child was a girl, she hid it well. For his part, Nepher loved the little girl, and she quickly became a favorite of both her mother and father. They named her Meritamen, which means "She who is beloved of Amun."

The name and the god who inspired it would not last long. As Nepher entered the third year of his reign, a new god, the Aten, was about to take center stage.

Chapter 8:

YEAR THREE

1349 BC, 3rd Regnal Year of Nepher's Reign, Thebes

No king ever held a Sed-Festival in the third year of his reign. It was unorthodox. It was unheard of. It wasn't done. Nepher did it anyway.

Sed-festivals were periods of renewal, a chance for the pharaoh to prove that he was fit to rule Egypt and a reassertion of his power. With the pomp of the coronation and the vibrant youth of a new pharaoh, a sed-festival in the first decade of the king's reign seemed superfluous. But Nepher felt it necessary to have one. He knew, from the beginning perhaps, that his reputation as a leader was shaky. A sed-festival would go a long way toward solidifying his position.

First, festivals were popular. They were exciting celebrations full of pomp and ceremony. The royal family handed out gifts and favors. They commissioned art and sculpture, built temples to commemorate the event. Artisans and merchants stood to make a lot of money from a sed-festival and the celebrations would attract foreign dignitaries and encourage the wealthy and powerful to spread their money around. Nepher, with his unusual appearance and abrasive personality could use a sed-festival to increase his approval ratings with the general populace.

Second, they were expressions of power. A sed-festival would prove that this new king was still the biggest man in Egypt. Nepher openly displayed his power through his wealth, his military, and his control of the religious cults. For a pharaoh who had squeaked into his job because of the power of his father, the festival was a chance for Nepher to prove he was powerful in his own right.

Finally, Nepher needed a way to introduce his new religious philosophy to the people, and there was no bigger way to announce a massive change in policy than through the planning and execution of a sed-festival. In the planning of this festival, Nepher signaled, in no uncertain terms, that Amun was no longer the most powerful god in Egypt. That distinction belonged to the Aten.

This shift in religious focus was the first major red flag to the Amun priesthood. The beginning of Nepher's reign had been relatively uneventful. The Amun priests knew that Nepher didn't like them very much (and liked their god Amun even less), but they had managed to retain their power, wealth, and influence in Thebes. Nepher allowed them to continue their "business as usual": to accept offerings, maintain their temples, and govern their "city within a city". Even though the Amun priests would have preferred Nepher's enthusiastic support, they could live with his indifference, as long as he didn't interfere in their affairs.

That was about to change. After almost two years of "staying the course" by completing his father's monuments, sticking with tradition, and playing politics at court, Nepher had had enough. He was ready to make the changes he dreamed of and usher in a new, exciting era of enlightenment. He was ready to tear down the existing structures, loosen the stranglehold that the old gods held on the empire, and return the office of pharaoh to ancient glory. The sed-festival was the first, bold statement of this new order.

Nepher commissioned the building of a massive new temple complex to rival Karnak and Luxor and to be completed by the time of the festival. The Great Temple of Amenhotep IV consisted of four main sections. The first was a temple to the Aten for the pharaoh himself. The second would be for his queen, Nefertiti, a place for women to worship the sun disc. There were two additional smaller temples, both of which were also dedicated to the Aten.

Everything about this temple complex was a departure from traditional religious structures. It was open to the air, its altars and offering tables exposed to the light of the sun. It emphasized the pharaoh and his wife, with no depictions of any of the other gods of Egypt's pantheon. The art and sculpture were in a style that could only be called revolutionary. And because of an innovative new construction method, the buildings seemed to rise up overnight from the floor of the desert.

In the layout and design of his temple, Nepher created a new kind of worship. Gone were the dark, cool, hidden rooms of Amun. Worshippers of the Aten drank in the sunlight as they worshipped in large open-air courtyards.

Offering tables and altars faced the sky. The temples offered little relief from the hot Egyptian sun, but the wealthy and influential employed their own fans and lightweight shaded pavilions. Common Egyptians had to sweat it out if they wanted to show their devotion to the pharaoh's new favored god. There were several enclosed spaces and storerooms, but the overall effect of the Temple of Amenhotep IV was bright, airy, full of the warmth and light from the sun.

Nepher called the largest and grandest structure the Gem-pa-Aten, "The Aten is Found." The main area of this temple was a huge courtyard surrounded by massive, square columns filled with scenes depicting the new pharaoh and his queen making offerings to the sun god. Colossal statues of Nepher and Nefertiti loomed over worshippers.

In addition to the Aten itself, the pharaoh and his wife were the principal objects of worship. Nefertiti, especially, held a place of high honor in the Temple. While the Gem—pa-Aten, the main structure, focused more on the pharaoh, Nefertiti had a temple all her own.

It was called the Hwt-benben, "House of the Benben Stone," and it was a temple built for female worshippers. In myth, the Benben stone was associated with the god Atum, one of the most ancient gods of Egypt and the first god in the Heliopolitan religious tradition. Like the Aten, Atum was a solar-deity connected with the setting sun, and he was believed to have created himself. He rose up from the dark waters of chaos at the beginning of time and rested on the mythical Benben stone. From his place on the stone, he brought forth the god Shu (air) and the goddess Tefnut (water), who went on to create the rest of the world. The similarities between Atum and the Aten are clear: two gods who created themselves and were able to act as both male and female to create all things on earth. The pharaoh's connection to the myth was further reinforced by associating himself with Shu and Nefertiti with Tefnut, thus completing, in the Hwt-Benben and the Gem-pa-Aten another divine triad—Aten, Nepher, and Nefertiti.

The Hwt-Benben was full of images of Nefertiti, and her role in the temple set her apart from every queen who came before her. Women in Egypt were an integral part of religious life, acting as priestesses, dancers, and musicians in most of Egypt's cults. However, some roles were reserved only for men, and even fewer were for the pharaoh. One of pharaoh's exclusive roles was to make offerings to the gods. Because of his inherent divinity, he was the only person qualified to communicate directly with the gods through offerings. In the Hwt-Benben, Nefertiti and her daughters broke with this tradition. On every wall, on every column, Nefertiti was resplendent in a long, blue wig and diaphanous robes, standing before an altar and doing what was heretofore unthinkable—making offerings to Aten, whose rays reached down to bless her and her tiny daughter, Meritamen, who stood just behind her.

These breaks with Egyptian tradition would have been shocking enough, but there were more, and these changes must have made a profound and lasting impression on anyone who came into the temple. The paintings, sculptures, and carvings were executed in an entirely new style. Gone were the idealized, traditional depictions of the pharaoh and his queen in their staid, lifeless poses. Gone were the traditional scenes of the stories of the gods. In their place, Nepher commissioned images that can only be called revolutionary. The pharaoh depicted himself with an almost grotesque exaggeration of his actual features. His face was cartoonishly long, his skull large and egg-shaped. His shoulders were narrowed and his arms and legs were spindly, elongated, and feminine. He accentuated the paunch of his stomach and his wide hips. Furthermore, his appearance was almost indistinguishable from that of his wife.

Nepher intentionally set his appearance apart from that of his ancestors and everyone else in Egypt. Because he believed that the Aten was the sole creator of all things, the Aten contained both male and female forces of creation. Nepher, by depicting himself in this androgynous way, highlighted his close relationship with the Aten. He carried this style over to his wife and (eventually) his children to set them apart as special members of the divine family. It was a small, elite group that no one else, not the priests, the nobles, and certainly not the commoners belonged to.

All of this dramatic change happened almost overnight. Nepher and his architects devised an innovative way to build the temple complex in record time. Instead of trying to move massive blocks of rock, as in generations past, Nepher's builders cut smaller bricks, called talatat blocks, from durable sandstone. These smaller bricks were much easier to work with and allowed the structure of the Gempa-Aten to be completed in less than two years. To the eyes of the wondering Egyptians, the Great Temple of Amenhotep IV rose up almost by magic.

Nepher built other temples to the Aten throughout Upper and Lower Egypt for the celebration of his unorthodox sed-festival. Each of these temples were constructed in the same revolutionary style using the same unorthodox methods. As preparations continued, it became clear that this sed-festival would be unlike any other. None of the traditional gods were honored, featured, or even mentioned——not Ptah, Osiris, Thoth, and certainly not Amun. Nepher did not run the traditional race course with the Apis Bull at his side. In fact, he didn't participate in any demonstrations of strength or skill at all. The purpose of this sed-festival was to introduce the people to their new god, their sole god, the Aten, and his only son, Nepher.

The elite of Egyptian society, from the military to the bureaucrats to the high priests, were alarmed and confused. Nepher, who had seemed to be following in his father's sensible, traditional footsteps, had, in the course of a year, upended everything. He wasn't interested in military strength or demonstrations of power; he refused to perform the rituals of his forebears (or, worse, gave them to his wife to perform), and he certainly wasn't afraid of the wrath of the traditional gods. Those who had lived comfortably for generations under the traditional power structure were now finding themselves in a precarious political position. Their wealth, their interests, possibly their actual survival, were all threatened by this odd-looking, unconventional upstart.

Something would have to be done about Nepher.

Chapter 9:

NEW MEN, NEW CITY

1348 BC, 4th Regnal Year of Nepher's Reign, Thebes

Nepher was justified in his desire to reform the systems of Egypt. He inherited a corrupt power structure filled with unqualified individuals who had achieved their positions through graft and influence-peddling. Self-interest, jockeying for power, and deals negotiated in the shadows were the norm. As a child, he had been pushed aside in this very system, his intelligence and vision ignored or mocked by the powerful elite. The high priests, especially, who were supposed to be holy men guiding their people to living in truth, or maat, had become something akin to conmen, seeking only to increase their own wealth and power. They took advantage of the faith and trust of the people, stole them of the fruits of their labor, and hoarded the spoils. To Nepher, they no longer served the gods, pharaoh, or the people.

Nepher trusted only a few close advisors and family members. He relied on his mother, Queen Tiye, and his uncle, Ay, to help him navigate the twisted political landscape in Thebes. Tiye managed the endless foreign dignitaries and needy vassal states. Ay kept the military happy, well-fed, and in line. Nepher also depended on Nefertiti, who took on more and more kingly responsibilities every day. They were a true partnership, and Nepher clung to her and their growing family. By Year Four of his reign they had three daughters, Meritamen, Meketamen ("Protected by Amun"), and Ankhesenamen ("Living through Amun"). Nefertiti had yet to bear him a son, but this disappointing development failed to diminish her power over the king.

Nepher's distrust of the traditional power structures led him to seek out fresh blood for the high positions in his court. He trusted only his handpicked advisors. Traditionally, a young pharaoh drew his lieutenants from the boys he grew up with—the sons of government officials who were raised and educated along with him in the royal nursery. But Nepher, ever the outcast, failed to build relationships with those young men. The old guard, no matter how experienced or qualified, were too set in their ways. So Nepher sought men outside the usual channels.

Nepher wanted to shape those around him, to teach them new ways of governing, inspired by the Aten and based on maat. As the pharaoh of the most powerful empire on earth, he found many willing and loyal disciples. One close aide took a name for himself that translates roughly to "Nepher is the reason I live." Nepher's royal chancellor, May, described himself as "a low-born man on both my father's and mother's side". He claimed that he was so poor before Nepher elevated him that he used to beg for bread. Even Ay, the king's uncle, praised Nepher's teachings, saying, "My Lord taught me, and I do as he instructs."

One of the most powerful positions in the new government was that of the High Priest of Aten. As pharaoh, Nepher was the de facto head of the cult of Aten; he was the only person able to communicate with the sun disc and was so closely associated with the god that there was little difference between Nepher and the Aten itself. However, as pharaoh, Nepher held many responsibilities outside of his religious position. There was an empire to run, after all, and Nepher needed the help of someone else to manage his new, all-powerful religion, to accept the countless offerings flowing into the temples, to maintain those temples, and to encourage and further the faith. The High Priest of Aten also served as a strong counterpoint to the High Priests of the other cults, especially that of Amun. Even though the Aten was the most favored of all the gods, it still needed a champion all its own at court.

Nepher selected for this most important office a man who became known as Meryre ("Loved by the sun god, Re"). Like most of Nepher's advisors, Meryre gained his position through the pharaoh alone. He was born under a different name, Meryneith ("Beloved of Neith," one of the earliest goddesses in Egypt), but changed it to better reflect the changing times and religious trends. Nepher loved and trusted Meryre and showered him with honors.

Park of Nepher's devotion to Meryre was because Meryre so avidly listened to Nepher's teachings and vision. Nepher said of his faithful servant, "I proclaim you Great of the Seers in the Temple of Aten…because you are in my heart. My servant, who hears my teaching, my heart is content with all that you are."

Nepher's teachings weren't limited to government. He guided painters and sculptors in his preferred artistic style, and there he found an eager audience as well, including the sculptor Thut, who created the Nefertiti bust. Bak, whose father had been the royal artist for Amenhotep, changed his whole way of painting at the guidance, instruction, and close supervision of his new master, Nepher. Even the new building methods using the smaller talatat blocks could be linked directly back to Nepher.

All of these changes, all of these reforms and new ideas threw the old guard into a frenzy. Every aspect of Egyptian life was changing under the new pharaoh, and wealthy and entrenched interests were finding themselves left out in the cold. The changes were felt in every corner of the empire, from the religious cults to Egypt's far-flung vassal states and allies.

Some of these old power players turned to Queen Tiye in the hopes that she might influence her son. The Mittanian King Tushratta, like many other foreign heads of state, believed at first that nothing much would change under Nepher. In a letter to Nepher early in his reign, Tushratta spoke warmly of Amenhotep and how sad he was that the old king had died. He went on to speak of the joy at hearing that Nepher inherited the throne.

"[Amenhotep] is not dead because [Nepher], his son, rules in his place. Nothing will change from how it was before…"

But everything changed, and soon Tushratta became frustrated with Nepher, who owed him two gold statues that Amenhotep had promised to give him as a bride price for one of his daughters. Nepher sent the two statues, but they were wooden ones, covered in gold leaf instead of solid gold. Tushratta appealed to Queen Tiye and their long alliance to try to get what was owed him.

"You know that I myself always showed affection to your late husband, and your husband showed affection to me. Let your son cause me no distress…Let him treat me ten times better than his father did."

Nepher had no time for these kinds of petty squabbles and, often as not, he ignored pleas from the old elite. This jockeying for money and power was exactly the kind of politics Nepher wanted to wipe out in his quest for truth and enlightenment.

He treated the High Priests, especially those of Amun, with equal disdain. He saw them as groping and manipulative, hoarding religious power and knowledge for themselves and trying to undermine the divine authority of the pharoah. At the beginning of his reign, Nepher tolerated the other religious cults and allowed them to continue practicing their rituals and ceremonies. Soon, however, he began to siphon funds from the cult of Amun, thus choking the cult and limiting its ability to keep its temples up and running. He used the money for his own projects honoring first Re-Horakhti and then the Aten.

The great god Amun didn't just lose money; he lost devotees, too. With the pharaoh so decidedly hostile to the old god, many noble and wealthy Egyptians "converted" their religious devotion from Amun to the new god in town, the Aten. Many took the lead of Nepher's new High Priest of

Aten, Meryre, and changed their names to reflect the new religious hierarchy.

The High Priest of the cult of Amun still held considerable sway, but he and his allies suspected that their days, and those of their god (and possibly all of the traditional gods) were numbered. He and his cohorts decided to take action. They found eager sympathizers in the members of the establishment who had been replaced by Nepher's band of nobodies, upstarts, and commoners. There was talk, whispered in the halls of the palace and the increasingly empty temples of Amun, that Nepher and his new way of doing things must be stopped.

What this resistance was or how Nepher discovered it is lost to history. Perhaps there was no actual conspiracy at all, and Nepher feared a threat that didn't exist. Even though Nepher may have been paranoid, he was not naive. Egyptian historians may have downplayed stories of betrayal or assassination, but a royal son would have been raised to watch his back against traitors and conspirators. And considering the religious revolution that Nepher was starting, he was wise to assume violent opposition from powerful enemies.

The religious center of Thebes was a challenging place for a king fighting against old, entrenched ways. The cult of Amun practically owned the city, and the old power structure was impossible to crack. Nepher realized by Year 4 of his reign, that if he and his family stayed in Thebes, he would never be allowed to achieve his dream of a enlightened nation devoted to Aten. At best, his reforms were doomed to fail in Thebes. At worst, he and his family would die at the hands of their enemies, and the 18th Dynasty would die along with them.

Egypt needed a fresh start. It needed a new city, a shining beacon where all of Egypt could worship the Aten through Pharaoh and his divine family. Nepher would build that city. He would leave the backwards traditionalists of Thebes behind and forge a new government and new state religion with his "new men"—his trusted advisors, loyal disciples, and beautiful wife. He would search for it himself, guided by his father the Aten, until he found the perfect place to usher in his era of enlightenment.

𓏲 𓅡 𓎟 ⸻ 𓊽

3200 Years Earlier, 1891 AD, Royal Tomb of Akhenaten, Amarna

Alessandro Barsanti was the first to find the royal tomb of Akhenaten, hidden deep within the cliffs to the east of the lost city of Amarna. Barsanti was an Italian Egyptologist who worked for the Egyptian Antiquities Service. He was thirty-four years old and heavy-set with a bushy mustache that was already turning grey. Even though some of the local Egyptians knew about the tomb, its distance from the city proper, about six kilometers, and the rough terrain to reach it had prevented other explorers from getting there. It was set far away from the private tombs of the other Amarna nobles and lay at the far boundaries of the city in what was called the Royal Wadi, the necropolis of Amarna.

The Amarna tombs differed dramatically from their counterparts in Thebes and elsewhere. First, the tombs were built to the east of the city. Everywhere else in Egypt, tombs were found in the west, where the sun "died" each day. Here in Amarna, these eastern tombs were the first places to greet the rising sun, almost as a challenge to death itself. Second, the artwork in the tombs had little in common with any that came before or after. Gone were images of Osiris, Anubis, and Hathor welcoming the dead into the afterlife. Gone was the Opening of the Mouth Ceremony that brought the dead back to life. In their place were depictions of the pharaoh Akhenaten, his wife, and their daughters. The only godly image was that of the Aten, the disembodied solar disc with its rays bestowing life to the king and queen. The Book of the Dead, the instruction manual for the afterlife that was customarily carved into tomb walls, was missing. In its place were scenes from everyday life or from nature, with odes to the divinity and majesty of the pharaoh and the Aten.

Barsanti had a good idea of who might have been buried in this remote tomb. The size and scope of it indicated its royal purpose. However, someone in antiquity had violated the tomb, scratching out the names and many of the images on the walls. The main funeral chamber's reliefs and cartouches were wiped out entirely. Two massive granite sarcophagi were smashed to pieces, their fragments left scattered over the floor of the main chamber. The damage to the walls and sarcophagi was brutal, systematic, and thorough. The bodies that had been laid to rest here were long gone, and Barsanti assumed that the coffins and the mummies had been desecrated and destroyed with the same ruthlessness.

In spite of the damage, the tomb was impressive. In a side group of rooms, Barsanti discovered that some of the paintings survived the vandals; he marveled at the intricate reliefs carved in the unique and now famous Amarna style. They showed the king and queen, under the rays of the Aten, mourning the death of a woman on a bier. A wet nurse, carrying an infant, stood to the side of this sad tableau. The baby was a member of the royal family, as signaled by the presence of two fan-bearers at its side. Similar scenes were found in these same side rooms, and Barsanti discovered an intact cartouche that identified the dead woman as Akhenaten's second daughter, Meketaten.

The layout of the tomb, like everything else associated with Amarna, was unorthodox. Not only was the tomb situated to the east of the city, but it was entered through a single, long corridor consisting of two sets of steps separated by a ramp. The corridor created a straight line from ground level all the way down to the burial chamber. This long, straight passageway seemed designed to allow the rays of the morning sun to reach all the way down to the king's final resting place. Even in death, Akhenaten sought the light of his father-god, the Aten.

The ruins of Amarna were originally discovered in the late 1700's, but it wasn't until the end of the nineteenth century that the city began to be understood by explorers and archeologists. At first, Amarna appeared to be just another ancient, ruined city, lost to the sands of the vast African desert. As archeologists like Barsanti explored the ruins, however, they discovered that the city had not fallen into ruin because of abandonment or neglect.

Like the mysterious tomb hidden deep within the eastern cliffs, Amarna had been intentionally dismantled. Someone had come into the city and razed it. Abandoned homes, like that of the sculptor Thut, were bricked up by residents who believed that they would someday return. They never did. Temples and palaces were stripped to their foundations as someone salvaged every scrap of usable material and took it out of the city. Everything that wasn't nailed down was pilloried, and whatever remained was vandalized in much the same way the tombs had been. Faces hacked off; names scratched out or written over. By the time archeologists rediscovered Amarna almost three thousand years after its fall, there was nothing left but a hint of the Royal Road that ran through the city and some lonely mud brick structures buried in the sand.

How could a city that was built for over 30,000 people disappear so quickly? And who would want to so utterly destroy it?

Chapter 10:

AKHENATEN

1347 BC, 5th Year of Akhenaten's Reign, 250km North of Thebes

To build a perfect city for the Aten, Nepher needed a virgin site, uninhabited, untainted by the old ways of doing things and unaffiliated with any of the old gods or traditions. Nepher's search led him northward 250 kilometers down the Nile, to a bend in the river that lay almost equidistant between Memphis, the traditional administrative capital of Egypt, and Thebes, its religious center. On a desolate windswept plain, bordered on the west by the life-giving Nile and on the east by steep, protective cliffs, he found his regime's new home.

Aten, it seemed, had written his name in the landscape. In the mountains above the site, there was a canyon that created a wide notch. Every morning the sun rose centered in this notch. It appeared huge on the horizon as it ascended into the desert sky, and the effect of the solar disc surrounded by the mountains created a naturally-occurring version of the hieroglyph for Akhet. Akhet symbolized the "horizon", a "mountain of light," the rising and setting sun. The Ahket was one of the glyphs in the cartouche for

Re-Horakhti, Nepher's preferred incarnation of the sun god at Karnak, and it was synonymous with the Aten. Nepher took this incredible coincidence as a sign that he had found the right place. This remote stretch of desert was where Nepher would build his great city of the sun. He named it Akhitaton, "The Horizon of the Aten," an apt name if ever there was one.

Nepher planned his city down to the last detail. He began by ordering the construction of large stelae. These were stone slabs, twenty five meters high, covered with art and inscriptions commemorating the founding of the city and recording Nepher's pronouncements about its purpose and plan. The stelae served as boundary markers that encircled the city. Everything in Akhitaton would be contained within the boundary stelae, according to a plan that Nepher proclaimed had been ordained by the Aten itself. The founding of a new city was cause for excitement and wonder throughout Egypt, and the energy, especially among Nepher's trusted elite was palpable as construction began.

Nepher, eager to connect himself and the new city directly with his father-god, the Aten, proclaimed (as recorded by the scribes on the boundary stelae):

"It is the Aten, my father, who guided me to Akhitaton. No official told me about it, nor any person in the whole land told me to make Akhitaton in this faraway place. It was the Aten, my father who advised me, so that Akhitaton could be made for him. I did

> not find it furnished with shrines or tombs...
> it did not belong to a god nor a goddess; it did
> not belong to a male or female ruler; it did
> not belong to any people...it was abandoned
> when I found it."

—after WJ Murnane, *Texts rom the Amarna Period in Egypt* (Atlanta 1995)

With this proclamation Nepher asserted that he alone was responsible for the founding, design, and construction of Akhitaton. No one else, and certainly no other gods or their cults, could ever lay claim or take credit for it. Akhitaton belonged to pharaoh alone. And in the city of the "Horizon of the Aten," only the Aten would be worshipped.

The design of the city originated from the placement of Nepher's tomb deep within the canyon to the east. The tomb was the focal point from which the city itself radiated out, much like the rays of the sun radiated from its rising in the mountain notch on the eastern horizon. Placing his royal tomb to the east of the city was received by some as a bad omen. Traditionally, Egyptians buried their dead in the west, especially west of the Nile, because the East, where the sun rises, was considered fit only for the living, while the west, where the sun sets, was the proper place for the dead. However, Nepher placed his tomb in the east to connect himself with his divine father, the Aten, as it rose to greet the day.

Once he chose a suitable site for his tomb, Nepher designated areas in the northern, central, and southern parts of the city as royal and religious focal points. At the far northern end of Akhitaton, Nepher built the North Riverside Palace with a lesser palace, the North Palace, just below it. These palaces were set apart from the other houses in the north, which belonged to the rest of the nobility, and the major administrative and religious temples that lay at the center of the city. The royal family, including the royal harem, took up their primary residence in these northern palaces.

The city administrators and artisans settled to the south of the city center, apart from pharaoh's family, harem, and the nobility. In these southern suburbs, the great military families and government officials built their homes, with the more fashionable and wealthy families living closer to the Nile. Thut, the royal sculptor, lived and worked in this part of town. As one traveled east, away from the river, the houses became smaller and shabbier, built for the less wealthy and connected. Even further to the east was a large workman's village, it's tiny structures a far cry from the glamorous houses, temples, and palaces along the Nile. Far south of the city, well below its center, Nepher built a special temple, called the Maru Aten ("The Viewing Palace of the Aten") as a retreat for his Lesser Queen Kiya. The establishment of this temple did not sit well with the Great Royal Wife, Nefertiti, and her daughters, as we will see.

The center of the city was a bustling hub. A focal point of the area was the Great Aten Temple, an impressive structure built in the same vein as the Gem-pa-Aten at Karnak. It was an enclosed, open-air temple surrounded by massive columns and filled with offering tables. The walls were painted with reliefs of Nepher and Nefertiti making their offerings to the city's only god, the Aten. Just south of the Great Temple were two official structures where the king and his court conducted government business, the Great Palace and the King's House. Another smaller Aten Temple lay just to the south of the King's House. It was called the Hwt-Aten, or Mansion of the Aten, and it was one of the first structures built in the city. Nepher used it as his primary place of worship while the Great Aten Temple was under construction and later converted it into a mortuary temple for himself. It aligned perfectly on an axis with the location of his tomb six kilometers to the east in the Royal Wadi.

Akhitaton was as much a city created to honor pharaoh as it was to honor the Aten itself, and a centerpiece of it was the Royal Road. This thoroughfare ran all the way from the pharaoh's main house at the North Riverside Palace, through the northern suburbs and into the city center where it widened into a square at the Great Aten Temple. It was a grand processional, thirty five meters wide and running the full length of Akhitaton all the way south to the Maru Aten. Each day the pharaoh and Nefertiti mounted their shining, golden chariot and, with their entourage, rode down the Royal Road from their palace in the north to the King's Palace in the city center. Their daily ride intentionally mimicked the progression of the sun as it crossed the sky. Pharaoh's adoring subjects lined the Royal Road and bowed, prostrating themselves before the royal family.

Nepher's vision for Akhitaton embodied the principles of maat, "living in truth". Gone were the idols to the old gods that made up the paintings, reliefs, and statues at places like Thebes and Memphis. In Akhitaton, nature was the primary inspiration for art, and the city was an idyllic and fluid merging of natural and manmade beauty.

Aten's Temples were open to the bright blue Egyptian sky. Gardens, watered by the city's plentiful wells, turned this arid stretch of desert into an oasis full of trees, flowering bushes, and exotic plants. Wildlife was abundant, both in the art and in the city, with artists painting flocks of ducks and cranes as they took flight from stands of papyrus and lotus flowers, the two plants most associated with the Two Kingdoms of Lower and Upper Egypt.

The most striking change in the art and style of Akhitaton was in the way pharaoh himself was depicted. Nepher wanted to record real life, not the old, stodgy idealized versions of his ancestors. Nepher and Nefertiti were painted playing with their daughters, kissing each other, and giving gifts to their friends and faithful followers. While their features may have been exaggerated to highlight their divinity and separateness from ordinary Egyptians, the scenes of their daily lives—eating dinner, lounging on cushions, and riding through the city on their chariot were almost ordinary and certainly not glamorous.

A city of the size and scope of Akhitaton needed supplies—food, wine, livestock, lime- and sandstone for building. Quarries to the north supplied construction materials. Farmland on the western side of the Nile grew abundant crops that were then ferried to the east to be enjoyed by Nepher, his royal household and the officials and dignitaries that streamed into the brand new city. The Nile, of course, brought everything else that could possibly be needed via barges and ferries, which hungrily drained resources from both Upper and Lower Egypt.

Nepher employed the building methods he perfected in Thebes to speed the construction of Akhitaton. The use of the small talatat building bricks, which had been so effective in the construction of the Gem-pa-Aten at Karnak, meant that workers were able to build structures quickly. Many of the homes of the poorer classes were hardly more than mud huts that could be built in less than a day from the dirt under the workmen's feet. With this wild frenzy of construction and creativity, the city was completed in less than four years. It was a towering achievement.

As the king and queen rode along their Royal Road each day in their dazzling chariot, they gazed with pride at the temples, palaces, houses, gardens and sanctuaries that they had manifested, with the blessings and help of the Aten.

As their vision for a new Egypt rose before their eyes, Nepher and Nefertiti wanted their own identities and those of their children to keep pace, so they changed their names to better honor the Aten. Nefertiti added to her birth name, becoming Neferneferuaten-Nefertiti, which means "Beautiful Are the Beauties of the Aten - A Beautiful Woman Has Come." Their daughters shunned their association with Amun and replaced his name with that of the sun god to become Meritaten, Meketaten, and Ankhesenpaaten. To change Nepher's name was more complicated. "Amenhotep," the name he had taken in Thebes to appease his father and the Amun priests was as out of place in his bright shining city as a dark, hidden Amun temple would be. So Nepher left behind his old identity as Amenhotep IV. He cast aside "Amen is satisfied" for the more appropriate "Effective on behalf of the Aten."

From the fifth year of his reign, he would forever be known as Akhenaten.

The city of Akhitaton may have been centrally located along the north-south axis of Egypt, but it was still isolated compared to the major cities of Memphis and Thebes. The topography of Akhitaton, with the Nile running through it on its western side and the forbidding cliffs to its east, contributed to the feeling of separation and isolation from the rest of the empire. Even though the king of Egypt and his court lived there, Akhitaton remained somewhat removed from the majority of Egyptian society. Akhenaten and Nefertiti didn't realize it, but they had built themselves a bubble. Surrounded by loyalists and a devoted military (kept in line by Ay), Akhenaten and Nefertiti shielded themselves and their children from any dissension that lay outside the city.

Akhitaton became a utopia for the faithful and loyal followers of the Pharaoh, and he showered his trusted allies with his favor. The king ordered the construction of a special place from which to bestow his largesse—a bridge over the Royal Road to connect the Great Palace with the King's House. The bridge was enclosed except for a large balcony, which became known as the Window of Appearance. This window allowed Akhenaten, Nefertiti, and their daughters to look out over their subjects on the Royal Road and, from there, to hand out gifts and favors. It was a festive, exciting time whenever the King and Queen appeared in the window as they gave out gold, jewelry, even articles of clothing to those members of the court who had particularly pleased them or performed a task well. To Meryre, the High Priest of Aten, Akhenaten and Nefertiti gave several elaborate golden necklaces. On Ay, the King's uncle, they bestowed many gifts, most notably a pair of red leather gloves. The Window of Appearance gave the people of Akhitaton yet another opportunity to gaze on their divine King and Queen and offer their praise, admiration, and fealty. In return, the king showered his loyal followers with the bounty of the Egyptian empire.

As the construction of Akhitaton proceeded at a feverish pace, Akhenaten and Nefertiti welcomed three more daughters to their happy royal family, Neferneferuaten Tasherit (Neferneferuaten "Junior" after her mother's new chosen name), Neferneferure ("The Most Beautiful of Re") and the baby of the family, Setenpenre ("Chosen of Re").

Nefertiti had yet to bear a son.

Chapter 11:

DISSENT

3300 Years Earlier, 1887 AD, Ruins of Amarna (Akhitaton), Egypt

The clay bricks weren't worth much after all, even though the old woman had spent hours digging them up and transporting them back to her village. She kept digging in the hopes that something of real value would emerge from the ground, but nothing did. Still, she could sell the bricks, with their strange markings, to someone who might find a use for them. They weren't worth much, but they were better than nothing, and she would get whatever money she could for them.

The man who bought the bricks thought they were fakes, simply because there were so many of them. He was used to the odd grifter or opportunist who tried to pull one over on him, but in this case, he decided to take a chance that these humble-looking clay blocks might be worth something. He offered the old woman a few cents for the lot, over three hundred in all. She was happy to be rid of them. At the very least, he might be able to pawn them off as actual antiquities to an unsuspecting collector. He lucked out and managed to sell them to another dealer who sold them on to the next and the next. Because they were (probably) worthless, no one took much care to preserve them. Sometimes one would drop and shatter to pieces on the ground. Sometimes, transported together, they rubbed against each other and lost their inscriptions and details. But that was okay, because there were so many of them… and they were worthless, after all.

Except they weren't. These clay tablets, 382 in all, dug up from the sands of what had once been Akhitaton, were one of the greatest archeological finds in modern history.

They became known as the Amarna Letters. They were written during the reigns of Akhenaten, his predecessor, and successors as a record of the international diplomatic history of the time, a diary of sorts, of the comings and goings and internal dealings between the powerful kings and military leaders of the New Kingdom. Unlike the "official" recorded histories of Egypt that were rife with exaggeration and were notoriously lacking in dissent, strife, or failure, the Amarna letters recorded actual events, actual correspondence. The Amarna letters were the truth. They were written in Akkadian cuneiform script, the commonly used diplomatic language of the day.

The Amarna Letters painted a picture of an ancient world heretofore hidden from history with all of the pettiness, squabbling, needling, flattery, charm, and groveling of high-level politics. They also provided the greatest insight yet into the mysterious reign of Akhenaten and life at the end of the Eighteenth Dynasty.

As archeologists pored over the Amarna Letters, a few things became clear. First, Egyptian politics was much messier than the "official" historical record let on. Second, there was a crisis of confidence among Egypt's allies and vassals when it came to Akhenaten and his reign. Finally, Akhenaten either didn't know what was going on in his own empire, or he didn't care.

3300 Years Later, 1347 BC, 5th Regnal Year of Akhenaten's Reign, Akhitaton (Modern Day Amarna)

Rib-Hadda wrote to Akhenaten again and again and again. At first, the letters were not too far out of the ordinary. Rib-Hadda updated Akhenaten on the usual squabbles and disputes that plagued the northen parts of the Empire. There was always an incursion from a warring tribe; the Hittites were always "knocking on the door"; other mayors and vassals could never be as loyal to Pharaoh as Rib-Hadda, and he was sure they were up to no good.

Akhenaten took these letters in his stride. Every day, it seemed, another messenger arrived from some far off, backwoods principality to plead a vassal's case for more money, more gold, more troops. The constant stream of needy, groveling messengers wore on Akhenaten. He greatly preferred when they arrived with reports of the good things that were happening in Egypt and its territories. It was even better when they arrived with money that he could use to build his city. Even though Akhenaten's primary focus was on the building of his new capitol, he also had ordered construction projects all over Egypt from

Heliopolis in the north to Soleb in the south. Akhenaten was much more eager for news about the progress on these projects under way in the "real" Egypt instead of squabbles in foreign places like Amurru in Syria.

Occasionally, at the urging of his uncle Ay, he would engage his military on a mission. For example, Akhenaten was willing to send troops to support the Nubian viceroy, the king's son of Kush, in the south during a campaign for gold and territory in Buhen and Amada. But for the most part, Akhenaten interested himself in domestic affairs. He strived to increase Egypt's independence from foreign states, not engage with them. International diplomacy exhausted him.

By the time Akhenaten had moved his court to Akhitaton, his allies had already grown frustrated with him, though they would never do much more than hint at their exasperation. Akhenaten was so very different from his father, Amenhotep, who not only engaged in foreign affairs but seemed to relish and enjoy the ins and outs of diplomacy. Not only did Akhenaten avoid diplomacy, he openly scorned it. So when Rib-Hadda's missives grew in urgency and fear, Akhenaten was inclined to ignore what was happening rather than face it head on.

Rib-Hadda was a vassal lord of Byblos, who became embroiled in a conflict with Abdi-Ashirta and his son, Aziru, rival leaders who ruled over the distant territory of Amurru in Syria. At first, Rib-Hadda may have been a bit hysterical about the threats posed to his territories, but his loyalties to Egypt and its pharaoh were clear. He had served faithfully under Amenhotep and relied on Akhenaten to treat his letters and messages with the same trust and careful consideration that Amenhotep had.

But as the situation in Byblos deteriorated, Rib-Hadda's letters became more urgent, more frequent and more dire in their reports:

> "I have repeatedly written to the palace regarding the distress afflicting me,...but no one has paid attention to the words that keep arriving. ...Send archers. The hostility toward me is great."
>
> —*EA 75 (KC Hanson after a translation by Mercer)*

> "...[Pakhura] has made gifts seducing the city against me, and woe to the place, she has become ungrateful. The city, which was not base in old times, is base to us."
>
> —EA 122 (Claude Reignier Conder, The Tell Amarna Tablets, 1893)

> "I have nothing. Like a bird that lies in a net. ...Furthermore, if the king is not able to rescue me from the hand of his enemy, then all lands will unite with Abdi-Ashirta. What is he, the dog, that he takes the king's lands for himself?"
>
> —*EA 79 (KC Hanson after a translation by Mercer)*

Akhenaten was unmoved by Rib-Hadda's pleas. In fact, he complained that Rib-Hadda asked for too much too often.

"You are the one who writes to me more than all the other vassals," he wrote with disgust in EA 124.

As the political situation deteriorated in the north, Rib-Hadda, already an old man, became sick. He lost his territories and was forced to live under the care of a neighboring vassal.

Betrayed and forsaken by his pharaoh, he wrote, "I am old and suffer from a serious illness. May the king, my lord, know that the gods of Gubla (Rib-Hadda's territory) are angry."

Letters like this should have been a warning to Akhenaten. In Egyptian life, everything was blessed or cursed by the gods. Military victories, the abundance of the crops during the growing season, the healthy birth of a child, the onset of disease and subsequent cure or death by it were all a reflection of the gods' approval or disapproval. Unrest in the North would not be looked upon by the rest of Egypt as just a disregard for military matters or even a simple sign of weakness. As the outer territories of Egypt were encroached on and started to fall, Egyptians began to wonder if they had angered the gods.

There was historical precedence for this belief as well. Several generations before Akhenaten came to power, the Hyksos had occupied large sections of the empire. In achieving Egypt's independence, the first pharaoh of the Eighteenth Dynasty, Ahmose, credited Amun with helping the Egyptians regain their land. Egypt had also, historically, been plagued by civil wars between the Upper and Lower Kingdoms. Ahmose credited the gods for uniting the two kingdoms and creating the greatest empire in the world. If military victories could be credited to the gods, then so could military defeats.

Akhenaten had connected himself so closely with one god, the Aten, that they were, for all practical purposes, the same being. If Akhenaten failed to protect a territory, then the Aten was to blame. If Akhenaten's troops were defeated, then the Aten must be weak as well. If allied Kings, mayors, and vassals lost respect for the Egyptian Pharaoh, then that pharaoh's preferred god was held responsible.

For Akhenaten, his disregard for military matters may not have seemed all that important to him. Perhaps he thought that allowing some territories to be lost would open up more resources for the remaining lands. It's possible that Akhenaten viewed theses vassal states in the north as more trouble than they were worth. If they couldn't look after themselves, then why should all of Egypt suffer to protect and defend them? After all, didn't they exist to build up and enrich Egypt, not drain it? Money was still flowing in from the majority of the empire; Egypt was still the wealthiest and most terrifying player in the entire known world. So what if a few cities filled with foreigners and barbarians fell under the rule of a rival state?

Akhenaten proved, yet again, that even though he was brilliant and ahead of his time in many ways, he failed to understand the importance of politics, and especially, public perception. Losing territory to an enemy may not have mattered much in actual impact on Egypt as a whole, but it corroded confidence in the king. And with all of the other changes happening in Egypt under Akhenaten and the new sole god of the Aten, Akhenaten could not afford to shake the confidence of his people any further.

Akhenaten's primary allies in Akhitaton at this time were the military, largely because of the influence of his Uncle Ay. Ay faced a challenging dilemma; Akhenaten's disregard for international and military matters was weakening Egypt's standing in the region. Akhenaten, at his uncle's urging, had secured the full, enthusiastic support of the military. In many ways, Akhenaten shifted the power that once belonged to the religious cults and the government bureaucracies over to the military. He honored the military in wall reliefs in the temples and throughout the city. He showered military leaders with gifts and favors. Akhenaten, in the capitol anyway, was popular among the armed forces.

However, the principal purpose of the military was to protect and defend the state. As the northern territories fell into chaos, as age-old enemies of Egypt began to slowly and inexorably encroach on lands long held by the pharoah, as foreign leaders began to ignore Akhenaten's demands for tribute or send letters of defiance and disdain, morale among the rank and file deteriorated. Nothing demoralized the armies more than losing, and Akhenaten was not only losing, he didn't even seem to want to win at all.

This deterioration in foreign affairs coupled with the radical new religious reforms caused serious strife throughout Egypt. The city of Akhitaton may have been an oasis of enlightenment, enthusiasm, wealth and growth, but the rest of

Egypt was increasingly skeptical or outright hostile towards the young pharaoh and his strange ways of doing things.

The cults that were marginalized by pharaoh took advantage of the people's skepticism and the weakening of their main rivals for power—the military, the Pharaoh himself, and his singular god. The Amun priesthood may have been weakened by the loss of offerings and the syphoning off of resources to the Aten, but they still held sway among the majority of Egyptians. Amun, after all, got the credit for saving the Empire only a few generations prior, and the cult's financial interests in agriculture, shipping and mining were responsible for thousands and thousands of people's livelihoods. If the High Priests of Amun could ally themselves with the other religious cults and convince the people that Pharaoh was misguided, just maybe they could wrest power back into their own hands. They could take advantage of the weakening of the military to both blame Akhenaten and forward their own cause among the people. They whispered in cities up and down the Nile that the gods were displeased with Akhenaten and were punishing Egypt because of the blasphemy of him and his wife, Nefertiti.

The Amun priests knew that they were in a war for the hearts and minds of the people of Egypt. At first, Akhenaten did not fully realize the danger he was in. He was certainly aware of the rumblings and dissent. It was the main reason he had moved his capitol from Thebes to Akhitaton. He may have even fled a downright coup. But he believed that consolidating power, pulling money from the cults, and ingratiating himself with the military would be enough to solidify his reign. It was not. More drastic measures were necessary.

If the Egyptian people continued to resist the Aten, if they refused to live in maat and respect the "natural" order of things, if they refused enlightenment in favor of tired, old tradition, then Akhenaten would have to force them into this new era. He would make them see.

Chapter 12:

OPPRESSION AND SUCCESSION

1342 BC, Regnal Year 9, Akhitaton (Modern Day Amarna)

By Year 8 of his reign, Akhenaten's city was nearly finished and was formally dedicated to the Aten. The royal court and bureaucracy had fully moved in. Finishing his great city gave Akhenaten the confidence to face his detractors head on. No longer would he tolerate dissent among his people. It was time to unify all Egyptians under the sole god of Aten. If Egypt were going to enter a new age of enlightenment and truth, all of the old traditions must be left behind and obliterated.

Akhenaten set his military and his trusted advisors on a campaign to wipe the other gods of Egypt out of existence. Because the Amun priesthood continued to be his rivals and, he believed, were conspiring against him, he was particularly ruthless in his rejection of Amun.

Akhenaten sent out the order. First, all references to Amun were to be wiped out. The military, still loyal to Akhenaten and closely connected to Ay, roamed Egypt smashing statues of Amun and his goddess wife, Mut. His hieroglyph was scratched out from cartouches and reliefs.

Even Akhenaten's father, Amenhotep, was not spared. Statues of the great king were preserved but the hieroglyph for Amun, an integral part of the old pharaoh's name, was chipped away, effectively wiping Amun from his role in Amenhotep's reign. The destruction was thorough, even the pylon at Karnak, over twenty meters high, was scaled so that the offending name of Amun could be removed from its top.

The persecution extended beyond just cartouches, wall reliefs, and statues. The High Priests of Amun, who had been struggling anyway since the beginning of Akhenaten's reign, began to really suffer. Akhenaten prohibited all offerings or tributes to any other gods but the Aten. He seized what little resources the Amun priesthood had managed to hold onto. Amun's estates and business interests were confiscated and transferred over to the new, sole god of Egypt, the Aten.

This persecution of the Amun might have been tolerated by the Egyptian people if it did not extend to all of the other gods of the Egyptian pantheon. No god but Aten was to be worshipped, and many ordinary Egyptians, who sincerely believed in their favorite gods and goddesses, found themselves forced to worship a god they neither understood nor particularly related to.

Part of this lack of religious affinity was because of the nature of the Aten itself, as envisioned by Akhenaten. The Aten was a disc set in the sky. It was faceless, voiceless, aloof, and it was connected to only the pharaoh. The Aten had no impact on the everyday lives of Egyptians. The solar disc may have been the source of all life on earth, shower-ing Egypt with its warmth, but to the Egyptians, it was a cold god who held nothing for them. They greatly favored their old gods, who were closer to real people living actual lives. The old gods had faces (even if they were the faces of animals); they married and had children. They fought with each other and loved each other. They mourned and celebrated. They died and came back to life and died again. The old gods understood what it meant to go through child-birth, to fight in a war, to be lonely and happy and angry. The Aten knew none of these things.

Not only was the Aten aloof and removed from the trials and tribulations of life, Akhenaten had decreed that the Aten could only truly be worshipped by the pharaoh himself. Atenism was, in many ways, a church with only one member, the Son of God as manifested by Akhenaten. The people of Egypt were not expected to really worship the Aten at all; Akhenaten wanted them to worship him, first, and secondly the royal family—his wife, Nefertiti and their daughters. Akhenaten replaced all of the images of the old gods with images of himself and his family. The Aten bestowed life and blessings on the royal family exclu-sively; it was up to the royal family to bless everyone else.

Akhenaten, in his zeal to reform the belief systems of Egypt, failed to understand how deeply rooted Egyptian faith was in the pantheon, and the people resisted giving up their beloved gods. Women refused to relinquish the small idols to Bes and Tawaret, the principal goddesses of child-birth. Fear of dying in childbirth (or of their babies dying) was real and could not just be wiped away with a royal decree. Gone was the pageantry of the great festivals where the statues of the gods sailed on magnificent barges down the Nile. In their place was the daily procession of Akhenaten and Nefertiti down the Royal Road, a cheap substitute that failed to nourish the people's spirits.

The changes to the religious structures had economic impacts as well. Money flowed into Akhitaton for the pharaoh's building projects and to support his court and his military, but the money had to originate somewhere. With the degradation of Egypt among its foreign tributaries and vassal states, Akhenaten began to raid the old cities of Egypt. Building and running his new city required massive amounts of money, and as rich as Egypt was, its wealth wasn't bottomless. Akhenaten used his new religion as an excuse to plunder the wealth of the other cults, taking their land, crops, businesses and resources.

Akhenaten took and took and took, but he didn't give in return. Many of the old cults supported their local economies including merchants, artisans, farmers, and bakers. By pulling resources into Akhitaton, the pharaoh was starving everyone else. The frustration expressed in the Amarna letters from the mayors, vassals, and allies of Egypt must have trickled down to the general citizenry as well.

Centralizing the religious and bureaucratic center of government had other problems. Akhenaten's "new men" were unfailingly loyal to him, but focusing so much power on so few led to widespread corruption and graft. Those who had the trust and ear of the king were able to extort or destroy their rivals and take advantage of those held in less favor. Some of Akhenaten's friends were sincere, true believers in their pharaoh, his reforms, and the Aten. Nefertiti was certainly one of these true believers. But others knew the power of flattery and how to work their way into the good graces of Akhenaten. They understood that he had been rejected as a child, and they knew that if they said the right things and acted in the right way that they could manipulate him.

These were the men who had managed to hold positions of power in both Amenhotep's court and in Akhenaten's. These were the men who changed their names and their faiths to go along with the new regime. They became Akhenaten's greatest enforcers and his biggest fans, but behind their smiles and flattery, there was only self interest. As long as Akhenaten kept them in power, as long as they were able to influence him for their own advancement, they would stand by his side. However, if the tables ever turned, so would they.

Ay, Akhenaten's uncle and brother to Queen Tiye, was such a man. He had spent his entire life at court and learned everything he needed to know about the ins and outs of the royal family from his father, Yuya, the commoner who had managed through skill and political intelligence to install his own children into the highest positions of power in Egypt. Ay had managed to not only be a closely trusted advisor of his brother-in-law Amenhotep, he had retained his power and standing under Akhenaten. Ay's close ties to the military gave him an advantage that almost no other advisor to Akhenaten had, and it was Ay that made sure the military was always favored, respected, and taken care of by Pharaoh. Ay understood that there were three primary pillars of power in Egypt—the royal court, the religious cults, and the military. He made sure that he had closely tied himself to at least two of these powers. And Ay had no intention of going down if the reign of Akhenaten should end in disaster.

The second of these shrewd, intelligent men was the High Priest of the Aten, Meryre. He knew how to sway with the political winds. He was from Saqqara in the north; his father had been a government official named Khaut. Meryre accompanied Akhenaten when the pharaoh established Akhitaton, and he showed his allegiance to the pharaoh and to the Aten by changing his birth name, which had been Meryneith, to Meryre. He built a magnificent tomb for himself in the northern cliffs east of the city. His tomb was more an homage to his king and mentor than to himself. Every wall proclaimed the glories of the Aten and showed scenes of the king and his wife worshipping the sun disc and receiving life from the god. Meryre chose to depict himself as a tiny thing compared to the king and his family.

The inscriptions on the walls read like a love letter to his lord and master, "…my excellent king who created me, who begat me, who made me grow, who associates me with princes, the Light by which I live, my Ka (spirit), day after day…"

This level of flattery must have gone over well with Akhenaten. He had nothing but praise for his faithful High Priest and bestowed on him some of the highest honorifics in Egypt, including Fan-Bearer on the Right Side of the King.

Meryre may have allied himself with Akhenaten out of genuine faith and affection, or he may have just seen an opportunity to advance himself and rise to a higher level of power than his father could ever have hoped to achieve. Whether he was a "true believer" or not, one thing was clear. He would not keep the name Meryre for his whole life—as the winds changed, so would he.

Akhenaten's sudden and violent oppression of other religious cults may have stemmed from several factors. First, as mentioned above, Akhenaten had finished the main construction on the city of Akhitaton; with the city formally dedicated to the Aten, perhaps Akhenaten had more time to turn his attention to the next phase of his transformation of Egypt. Maybe he felt pressure from his political allies and diplomats to show some kind of interest in the empire at large and so sent out decrees as a way to reassert some of the power and prestige he lost because of his apathy in military affairs. Maybe he needed more money. Akhitaton was hungry for resources, and the king may have decided that he didn't much care if other cities and territories suffered a loss of their wealth as long as Akhitaton, which was essentially a massive offering to the Sun God, was well fed and kept.

Another event occurred around Year 9 of Akhenaten's reign, and this event may have boosted the pharaoh's confidence in his longevity. This event would guarantee the continued influence of the Aten after his own death.

Akhenaten finally had a son.

He named the boy, Tutankhaten ("Living Image of the Aten"), and the child became heir to the throne of Egypt. It isn't clear who the mother of the boy was, but it was neither Nefertiti nor Kiye, the two principal wives of Akhenaten. All that is known is that the boy's mother was a member of the royal family, probably a sister or a cousin of Akhenaten himself.

Akhenaten was overjoyed at the birth of his heir, because now he could look to the future beyond his own life span. With the birth of Tut, the Eighteenth Dynasty would continue and the religious reforms and worship of the Aten would be sure to outlive the father. Akhenaten would teach his son all the ways of the Aten, and some day, Tut would become the second living embodiment of the sun god, when Akhenaten went to join his heavenly father in the sky.

The birth of a son must have sent a shockwave through the royal harem, especially with Nefertiti and her daughters. Akhenaten's future dynasty was bolstered by the birth of Tutankhaten, but the birth of an heir to another woman in the harem could only be a bad sign for Nefertiti's own fortunes. She was still the Great Royal Wife, and by all accounts Akhenaten still loved her and held her in the highest esteem, but she would never be the Mother of the King. Once her husband died, all of her status and titles would die with him. For a woman who had been ruling Egypt as almost an equal to her husband, it was a catastrophe. To her father, Ay, it forced him to reevaluate his own position at court because he, too, stood to lose power once Akhenaten died. Without a son, Nefertiti would need to find another way to cement her position into the future, especially if she survived her husband.

She had several options. First and foremost, she would need to connect one of her daughters to the young crown prince. One of her daughters (Tut's half sisters) would have to marry Tut as soon as possible. Second, she would have to do more to ingratiate herself with Akhenaten. If she could somehow convince him to make her co-regent, then she would have more control over how the succession was managed after he died (assuming, of course, that Akhenaten died first). Third, even though she had so firmly connected herself to the religious philosophy of Akhenaten, she needed to branch out and make allies outside the close inner circle of the king. Her father, Ay, with his connections from the reign of Amenhotep and his friends in the military, would be of help here. Finally, she would need to eliminate any further threats from inside the royal harem itself. She was not the mother of the Crown Prince, but she was still the Great Royal Wife, and she needed to maintain and bolster that position at all costs.

Nefertiti's greatest rival in the harem had always been Kiye, the cute and mischievous "Monkey" who had charmed Akhenaten. Nefertiti was worshipped as a goddess, regal and aloof, but Kiye held her own place of honor in the king's heart. He built Kiye a temple of her very own in the southern part of the city, called the Maru Aten, and she was not only allowed to participate in religious ceremonies alongside her husband, but she even offered to the Aten on her own. No woman other than Nefertiti shared such an honor. The sculptor Thut created busts and statues of Kiye much like the one he had sculpted for Nefertiti, and in paintings and reliefs Kiye was sometimes depicted at almost the same scale (and status) as Akhenaten. Nefertiti and Kiye are even shown wearing the same style of Nubian wig, a testament to their comparable status.

At some time in the Twelfth Year of the Reign, Kiye disappeared, and it is clear that her disappearance came with a certain level of disgrace. The casket and canopic jars originally intended for her burial were never used by her. Her mummy was never found. But most tellingly, someone scratched her name and images from the walls at Maru Aten and the other temples where she had held a place of honor with her husband. In some places, Kiye's name was replaced by those of Nefertiti's daughters, Meritaten and Ankhesenpaaten. Not only had her name and images been erased, but she became connected to a story of an unfaithful wife who betrayed her husband in spite of his great love for her. Had the free-spirited Monkey actually been unfaithful or had she fallen victim to a vicious rumor circulated by a jealous Nefertiti?

Regnal Year Twelve saw the fall of Kiye, and the loss of this charming young woman at court wouldn't be the only tragedy of that year. Akhenaten's campaign of religious oppression throughout the rest of Egypt was entering its third year. Egypt had begun to lose its status with its allies. Resentment among the people outside of the capitol city grew. But inside the city, everything was still bright. The Aten rose on the eastern horizon to bless the pharaoh, his wife, and their daughters. The pharaoh, in turn, set out every day on the Royal Road to greet his adoring subjects, who groveled at his feet. There was finally an heir, a crown prince who would some day carry on the tradition as the divine son of the Aten and Pharaoh of the Two Kingdoms. In the king's paradise of Akhitaton, all was right with the world.

Chapter 13:
TRIBUTE

Circa 1900 AD, Tomb of Ay (Tomb 25), Modern Day Amarna

Ay's tomb at Tel el Amarna was already badly damaged by the time Norman de Garis Davies, an Egyptologist with the Egypt Exploration Fund's Archaeological Survey, entered it to study the famous inscriptions on the south wall of its entrance corridor. The tomb was first explored by the collector and Egyptologist, Robert Hay in the mid-1800s. Over the ensuing decades, the tomb had been vandalized and raided, but before the damage, it's impressive size and magnificent reliefs made it the most beautiful and grand tomb of Amarna.

Nevertheless it was unfinished, and Davies wondered why this tomb, like all of the Amarna tombs, was never completed. There seemed to be no historical reason for it. Construction on most of them began well before the end of the reign of Akhenaten or the abandonment of Akhitaton, but for some reason, later in the reign, around Regnal Year 12 and after, all construction ceased. Most record-keeping of any kind was lost to history after Year 12, and the mystery of the last five years of Akhenaten's reign plagued Egyptologists like Davies and his colleagues.

Ay himself was never laid to rest in this tomb, although it would be used for other burials after the desertion of Akhitaton. When the tomb was first discovered, it was filled with these later burials as well as debris and broken pottery, all of which took almost ten years to sift through and clear out. Ay's actual final resting place was back in Thebes, on the west bank of the Nile in the Valley of the Kings in a tomb that was discovered in 1816 by Giovanni Belzoni and became known as WV23. WV23 gave the valley that contained it the name Valley of the Monkeys because of the distinctive baboon paintings on its walls.

Why Ay had two tombs, one in Akhitaton and one in Thebes, and the ensuing events that would lead him from Akhitaton back to Thebes was a story of political survival that would be uncovered over the next century. But for the time being, Norman de Garis Davies was principally interested in the extensive inscriptions on the south entrance wall and what they told him about this unusual period in ancient Egyptian history.

Davies had made his life's work the study of hieroglyphs and wall paintings in the tombs of Egypt. He spent months in the Amarna tombs, painstakingly recording wall inscriptions and copying paintings using a technique he and his wife, Nina, created for the Metropolitan Museum of Art in New York. The inscriptions in Ay's tomb were some of the most important and unique in all of Egypt, and Davies was determined to capture them before they sustained any further damage.

The inscriptions were a poem, possibly a song, and most archeologists agreed that it was written by pharaoh himself,

The Heretic King, Akhenaten. *The Great Hymn to the Aten* was a beautiful tribute to pharaoh's faith in the solar disc, a song of worship but also a religious manifesto outlining the main ideas and beliefs of this unorthodox religion. De Garis Davies recognized its similarities to many of the psalms in the bible, which fueled theories that Akhenaten may have been the first monotheist in history and maybe even the ancient historical figure of Moses.

De Garis Davies gazed in wonder at the inscriptions, which were considered one of the greatest literary achievements of the ancient world, alongside such famous works as the Iliad, the Odyssey, and the much older Epic of Gilgamesh. Its imagery and language captured not only the king's faith but also the unique connection between the religious and political realities of his time.

> *"Thou are in my heart,*
> *And there is no other that knows thee*
> *Save thy son Neferkheperure WaenRe (Akhenaten),*
> *For thou hast made him well-versed in thy plans*
> *and in thy strength.*
> *The world came into being by thy hand,*
> *According as thou hast made them.*
> *When thou hast risen they live,*
> *When thou settest they die.*
> *Thou art lifetime thy own self,*
> *For one lives (only) through thee."*
> —Hymn to the Aten

The beauty of the verses masked their political implications. In the *Hymn of the Aten*, the disc of the sun was all powerful, the fount from which all life sprang. When the sun shone on the land, all living things were blessed, and when it disappeared into the west:

> "All their goods which are under their heads might
> be stolen,
> (But) they would not perceive (it).
> Every lion is come forth from his den;
> All creeping things, they sting."

For Akhenaten, there was only one god and the absence of this god during the hours of the night when he was hidden from sight, were dangerous—full of threats, hidden perils, and treachery.

De Garis Davies was strangely moved by this hymn to the sun god. Davies himself was a minister of the Congregational Church in England, and he couldn't deny the similarities between Akhenaton's hymn and the psalms of the Christian bible. They were so similar, in fact, that Davies almost believed he was reading the original source material for the Book of Psalms. But whether or not this incredible work influenced future writings, the *Hymn to the Aten* was the crowning achievement of a pharaoh who was far ahead of his time. Akhenaten was the first monotheist, a religious tradition that would span thousands of years and become the primary belief system of three of the most widespread religions in the world—Judaism, Christianity, and Islam.

Why, then, did the ancient Egyptian people have such a difficult time accepting Akhenaten and his ideas when they would later prove to be so popular and durable?

𓆣 𓏶 𓅢 𓀢 𓏭

1339 BC, Regnal Year 12, Akhitaton (Modern Day Amarna)

In the twelfth year of his reign, Akhenaten called together "the chieftains of every foreign land" to come to Akhitaton for a tribute festival. The full force of Akhenaten's reforms had been in effect for three years. The campaign to obliterate the old gods and religious cults was well established, and the people of Egypt were afraid to be discovered with even small totems to the old gods, especially those of Amun. The hieroglyph for the word "gods" had been excised from use, because in the new state religion, there was only one god, the Aten. Even the Egyptian word for "mother" was changed because it was too closely related to "Mut", the name of Amun's wife.

The Aten's full name and titles, before Regnal Year 9 had included the names of Re, Harakhti and Shu, but during the purge of the old gods, even Aten's name changed. Harakhti and Shu were removed, while only Re remained. Aten's new full name, significantly, was written in two cartouches, like the pharaoh's. The message was clear: the Aten and the Pharaoh were, for all intents and purposes, the same being.

By calling all of his foreign vassals to Akhitaton, the king was able to accomplish a few important objectives. First, tributary festivals of this kind were a fantastic way to bring in a lot of money and resources in a short period of time. Egypt was beginning to sag under the weight of Akhenaten's excesses, and the fast inflow of cash and goods from the foreign states would go a long way to replenishing the coffers. Past tributes of this kind attracted thousands of men, all laden with gold, silver, rare spices, incense, and exotic animals.

By Year 12, the resentment and frustration that had been brewing under the surface in the diplomatic sphere was boiling over into open hostility. The tribute festival was a way to remind the foreign vassals of Egypt's continued military dominance. Bringing foreign heads of state into Akhenaten's capitol, onto his turf, made them easier to control, manipulate, and to remind them of exactly who was boss. The king required his subordinates to attend the festival. If they could not attend in person, they were expected to send someone near and dear to them, their sons in their fathers' stead or their daughters, who would be welcomed into the pharaoh's harem. These "guests" were little more than hostages, to be held in the city as an insurance policy against treachery or rebellion.

Finally, the festival of foreign tribute was an opportunity to further "sell" the new monotheism to the people on the outskirts of the empire. The city of Akhitaton was impressive, and the conspicuous wealth, power, and prosperity must have appeared glamorous to the foreigners who came to visit. The receipt of foreign tribute allowed people from all over the empire to interact with one another, and perhaps Akhenaten was trying to further his belief that the solar disc, by shining equally all over the world, could be a unifying force among all of the different peoples of Egypt.

Of course, a fabulous party, especially one that the "guests" are expected to pay for, is no substitute for diplomacy or economic and military support. The foreign vassals who attended were there, not because they sought enlightenment or even connection to the heart of the Egyptian government. They had traveled to Akhitaton under duress and in the hopes that appearing directly before the king might gain them some political advantage to take back home.

While the festival of foreign tribute achieved certain objectives of the king, it couldn't solve the growing problems facing Egypt. The people were demoralized and spiritually adrift. They were unable to understand or connect to their new god and unwilling to fully let go of their old ones. The displaced priests of the now-defunct religious cults seethed in the shadows and whispered, "What can be done about Akhenaten?" The military, which had at first allied itself with the new regime, was having its own doubts as the trouble in the northern territories grew worse and Pharaoh seemed completely disinterested in the threats facing the country.

Akhenaten didn't realize it, but he had created the perfect storm for his own demise. He systematically alienated every potential ally until there were almost none left. He had taken away his people's faith as well as their prosperity. They could no longer even feel safe as foreign enemies smelled blood in the water and encroached on the borders.

The reign of Akhenaten had reached a tipping point, and the festival of foreign tribute may have been the final straw, because along with all of the gold, silver, and exotic animals, the foreign vassals brought something else to Akhitaton.

They brought the plague.

𓏏 𓅂 𓃗 𓃂 𓏏

Kiye was not the only member of the royal household to die in Regnal Year 12, and the festival of tributes may have been one of the last times that Akhenaten and Nefertiti's family were all together.

Even though Nefertiti never bore Akhenaten a son, their family of daughters were a great joy to them. Some of the most touching and beautiful paintings of the time are of the royal daughters with their parents. The six girls, born over ten years, were seen embracing their mother and father, participating in religious ceremonies, sitting on their father's lap or playing with their mother's earrings.

But after Regnal Year 12, some of the daughters disappeared from the historical record. Meketaten, whose death is depicted on the walls of the royal tomb of Akhenaten, seems to have died in childbirth, but the two youngest girls, seen in the paintings depicting the Twelfth Year Tribute, disappear completely after that.

Whether the foreign tribute was the actual cause of the plague that came to Akhitaton is unclear, but around this time a disease did ravage the area, taking the lives of rich and poor alike. Kiye and Akhenaten's two youngest daughters may have fallen victim to it. Perhaps even Meketaten had been effected before the birth of her child.

There was another possible casualty of this plague who died around this time, and her death would signify the end of an era, and, quite possibly, the beginning of the end of Akhenaten's reign. Queen Tiye, who had reigned over the most prosperous and peaceful era in Egyptian history with her husband Amenhotep the Magnificent, passed away in the Twelfth Regnal Year of her son.

The death of so many loved ones in such a short time devastated Akhenaten and Nefertiti. The beautiful life they had created for themselves was shattered. Their shining city fell victim to disease and death. Night, which had already fallen on much of the Egyptian empire, had finally come to the city of the sun.

Chapter 14:
THE CONSPIRACY

1335 BC, Regnal Year 16, Akhitaton (Modern Day Amarna)

By Year 16, the writing was on the wall for everyone associated with the court of Akhenaten, even if Akhenaten could not see it. Sixteen years of financial excesses, religious fanaticism and oppression, and diplomatic apathy had left the great Egyptian empire on the brink of collapse. Something absolutely had to be done about the Pharaoh.

The suffering of Egypt was at its worst in the outer reaches of the empire and in the former religious center of Thebes. In the northern outskirts, opportunistic foreign invaders were picking off cities and territories like lions hunting gazelles. They sought the weakest outliers and went in for the kill, confident that no troops or archers would be sent from any of the strongholds on the Nile.

Thebes, once the beloved residence of Amenhotep the Magnificent and the wealthiest city in the empire, had fallen into neglect and disrepair. The great temples at Karnak and Luxor had been shuttered for over eight years and took with them most of the wealth of the city. The disgraced Amun priests who resisted the oppression of the Aten were in hiding. They believed that their god had not only forsaken them but had abandoned all of Egypt because of the heresy of the pharaoh. Every misfortune, every setback, every illness was blamed on Akhenaten. Because Akhenaten turned his back on the true protector of Egypt, Amun-Re, the great god turned his back on the Egyptian people.

One devotee of Amun lamented:

> "Come back to us, O lord of continuity! You were here before anything came into being, and you will be here when they are gone. As you have caused me to see the darkness that is yours to give, make light for me so that I can see you. As your ka (spirit) endures and as your beautiful, beloved face endures may you come from afar and allow this servant...to see you! ... Oh Amun ... may you drive off fear!"

—(after AH Gardiner, Journal of Egyptian Archeology, 1928, and WJ Murnane, Texts from the Amarna Period in Egypt, Atlanta 1995)

Even the northern cities, whose affiliations with Re had spared them some of Akhenaten's wrath, were struggling under an economy that forced them to send exorbitant amounts of money to a city 200km to the south that was widely regarded as a vanity project for a lunatic.

Someone had to restore order before it was too late and the Egyptian empire fell into civil war, open rebellion, or occupation by foreign hostiles. But who? Short of staging an actual coup against the pharaoh, who could convince him to change course? Akhenaten had always been a man who believed fervently in his own ideas. Being Pharaoh made him also a god, and in his religious view, he (with his father the Aten) was the *only* god. How could such a man be convinced that he had miscalculated? How could he be encouraged to change? Who would be willing to risk their own lives by challenging him, even if it meant saving Egypt?

By this time in Akhenaten's reign, the Amun priests had nothing to lose. Their temples were in ruins; the name of their god had been excised from history; their idols were smashed. They were destitute and outcast. Despite their sorry state, they still had sympathizers and devotees who secretly supported them. And as the situation in Egypt deteriorated, some of these sympathizers were ready to stand up to Akhenaten and put an end to his heretic regime.

The problem with the Amun priesthood was that none of them or their allies could get anywhere near the king. Whatever the incident was in Akhenaten's fourth regnal year that had encouraged him to flee Thebes and establish the city of Akhitaton, it had made him paranoid, especially of anyone associated with Amun. The Amun priesthood would never be able to get close enough to the pharaoh to threaten him, much less engage him in a conversation about changing his political and religious policies.

Akhenaten trusted few people in general, and almost none of them had any kind of relationship with the Amun priests. These were the "new men", after all, a tiny, insular circle. They were "true believers" either in the Aten or the Pharaoh or both; many of these men owed Akhenaten not just their positions and their power but their very lives.

If Akhenaten fell, they would fall, too. The only way to change course was to convince one, or perhaps several, of these close advisors to go against their pharaoh. It was a tall order.

Anyone willing to betray Akhenaten was putting their lives on the line. If they failed in their efforts to thwart the king, they would certainly be disgraced, exiled, or worse. But if they failed to act, Egypt might descend into economic collapse, a religious civil war, or tribal anarchy. Whatever the final outcome, Akhenaten's loyalists risked finding themselves on the losing side. The only way to protect themselves was to somehow play both sides against the middle, so that they could survive, no matter who came out on top—Akhenaten or the Amun priesthood.

Akhenaten could not possibly have anticipated who would be the ones to eventually betray his crusade. They were so closely tied to him and his regime that it was inconceivable that they would suddenly go to work for the other side. His complete trust in them is what made them such a threat; they were the perfect conspirators, above suspicion and above reproach. They had never acted in any way that might hint at what was to come. They were more than his subjects, or even his loyalists. They were his friends. They were his family.

The three people who would do the most to end the age of Aten would be the three most responsible for creating it in the first place: Nefertiti, the Aten High Priest Meryre, and Akhenaten's uncle and father-in-law, Ay.

How Nefertiti finally convinced Akhenaten to make her co-regent is unclear. It's possible that she never actually held the title of Pharaoh, though many Egyptologists now believe that her sudden disappearance from the historical record is not because she was disgraced or died but because she changed her name when she rose to the co-regency alongside her husband. Akhenaten had always exalted Nefertiti. Among Great Royal Wives, who usually wielded a certain level of power and prestige, Nefertiti was something more. From the beginning of their marriage and their reign, Akhenaten made her almost an equal in everything. She fulfilled all of the offices of the pharaoh, including the religious ones. She was depicted riding in chariots, smiting enemies, and bestowing favors. In carvings and reliefs, she was almost as tall and powerful as her husband, and she wore the uraeus just like the pharaoh. So maybe it wasn't such a leap when, in the last year of Akhenaten's life, he turned the reins of power over to her.

There is a relief carving of Akhenaten with his co-regent that shows them kissing affectionately. For this co-regent to be a man would have serious implications, and for a while archeologists suspected that Akhenaten might be bisexual. The more reasonable explanation is that this co-regent is Nefertiti, who has finally been elevated to full and equal ruler with Akhenaten.

Her new name was Ankhkeperure-Neferneferuaten. Almost as soon as she took office, the stranglehold that the Aten religion had held over the people for the last fifteen years began to loosen. In Thebes, the priests of Amun were permitted to begin worshipping their god again, albeit on a limited scale that was nothing like they had in the past. The return of the old gods wasn't exactly encouraged, but it was no longer forbidden. It was a tiny step forward in healing the wounds of the recent past.

How Akhenaten felt about this change in policy is unclear. Maybe, by this time, he was so far out of touch that he didn't even know these reforms were happening. Like his father before him, he had grown fat and lazy. There is evidence that in the later years of his reign, he married his own daughters, much the way Amenhotep had. The death of three of his children and his mother in Year 12 as well as the constant resistance to his reforms took much of the fire and passion out of him. Perhaps, like his father before him, he was content to sit back and enjoy himself in the city he had built and let his wife take over governing for a while.

Nefertiti was happy to oblige. Because she never bore a son, her only path to power was to become pharaoh herself. If she managed to outlive Akhenaten, and it appeared she would, she and her father Ay would have a lot to say about who became the next pharaoh of Egypt. The Crown Prince Tutankhaten was only eight years old. This tiny boy was the only person standing in Nefertiti's and Ay's way.

There is one more important figure during this time, whose emergence and role are shrouded in mystery. He is the man (or woman) who would become pharaoh immediately after Akhenaten and Neferneferuaten. His name was Smenkhkare.

𓏺 𓅡 𓃗 𓌾 𓏺

3300 Years Later, 2010 AD, KV 55, Valley of the Kings

Dr. Zahi Hawass, the most famous Egyptologist of the modern era and Egypt's Secretary General of the Supreme Council of Antiquities, was determined to solve the mystery of the mummy in KV55 as part of a scientific initiative called the King Tutankhamun Family Project. Over one hundred years after the initial discovery of KV55, there was still speculation and disagreement about who lay in the broken and defaced golden coffin. Most experts agreed that the mummy was a male, but its age, cause of death, and place in history were still a riddle.

The conventional wisdom at the time was that the remains belonged to the mysterious Smenkhkare. Much of the dating of the mummy's age placed him in his early twenties at the time of death, too young to be Akhenaten. That would make Smenkhkare a potential younger half brother to Akhenaten (with Amenhotep as their shared father) or maybe a much older half brother to King Tut (with Akhenaten as the father). The mummy's physical similarities to Tut (the elongated skull, especially) indicated a close familial relationship. If the mummy was proven to be under the age of thirty when he died and was confirmed to be male, then it must be Smenkhkare.

Smenkhkare made a brief appearance in the history of ancient Egypt when he reigned for a short time immediately after the death of Akhenaten. There was no mention of him before or after his one or two years as Pharaoh. Theories abound about who exactly he was. He is known to have been married to Akhenaten and Nefertiti's eldest daughter, Meritaten, which would indicate that Smenkhare was an older son born to a lesser wife with Akhenaten. He may have been Kiye's son, which would explain why Kiye held such a place of honor in Akhenaten's harem. Perhaps he was the son of one of Akhenaten's foreign wives, which would make him less desirable as an heir but still an option when it became clear that Nefertiti would not produce a boy of her own. Some Egyptologists theorized that Smenkhkare was none other than Nefertiti herself, who for some reason had changed her name twice as regent—first to Neferneferuaten then to Smenkhkare. Both of these pharaohs carried the same prenomen, Ankhkheperure, a clue that they might be one and the same person.

Whoever he (or she) was, Smenkhkare disappeared from history after no more than two years as pharaoh. He was succeeded by another minor king who eventually became the most famous in Egyptian history, King Tut.

If the remains in KV55 belonged to Smenkhkare, some of the mystery of the final years of Atenism might be solved, but the real find would be the mummy of Akhenaten himself. The exaggerated depictions of him in Amarna—with his enormous skull, spindly limbs, and wide hips—raised many questions about his overall health and genetic makeup, which could only be answered by finding his body. There was a large contingent of Egyptologists who believed that the remains in the tomb were his. The physical similarities between Tut and the KV55 mummy could just as easily be shared between father and son as between half-brothers.

By 2010, Akhenaten's mummy had yet to be found or identified; almost none of the royal family from the Amarna period were seen or heard from after the fall of Atenism. The mummies of Queen Tiye, Kiye, Akhenaten, Smenkhkare, Nefertiti and her daughters were all missing. With so many lost mummies from this era, archeologists argued that the bodies of individuals associated with the reign of Akhenaten were intentionally destroyed in antiquity, hacked to pieces and scattered in the desert. Dr. Hawass disagreed. He believed that the mummy in KV55 belonged to a close relative of Tut, and he set out to solve the mystery once and for all.

Ever since the first explorers entered the mummies' tombs, legends arose of the Curse of the Pharaoh. Any bad luck to befall an archeologist or Egyptologist was proof that the mummies, with their ancient mystical powers, jinxed anyone who dared disturb their eternal rest. There were famous examples of explorers who fell prey to "the curse." Lord Carnarvon, the famous English aristocrat who funded Howard Carter's discovery of King Tut's tomb in 1922, fell victim to Tut's curse when a mosquito bite caused an infection that ended his life shortly after the tomb was opened. Howard Carter himself was troubled by the curse when, on the same day he found Tut's tomb, a cobra slithered into his house in Egypt and killed his beloved pet canary. Any time something went wrong around the opening of a tomb or the exhumation of a mummy, Pharaoh's Curse was to blame.

Aside from the absurdity of a such a "curse" in general, the pharaohs of Egypt would not have wanted to be left in obscurity. For a mummy to reemerge in the modern era after thousands of years and become famous again was exactly what the ancient pharaohs intended. It was why they recorded their names in the lists of kings, built statues and temples dedicated to themselves, and took such care with their tombs and burials. Being remembered forever was a form of eternal life.

Nevertheless, stories of the Mummy's Curse persist, and as Dr. Hawass conducted his experiments on the mummies as part of the King Tutankhamun Family Project, strange things happened. Hawass and his driver almost struck a little boy on their way to one of the tombs. A car transporting a high tech scanner broke down before reaching the King's Valley. When the scanner finally arrived, the city power in Luxor blacked out before it could be used. Brand new machines malfunctioned, taking hours to fix. Freak rain and windstorms kicked up in the arid Egyptian desert. As Dr. Hawass labored to reveal the mummies' identities to the world, to try to piece together Tut's family, there were complications at every turn.

Perhaps the Curse of the Pharaoh was working in reverse, at least in the case of KV55. Whoever cursed this mummy as the "Evil One" did not want Dr. Hawass to find out who he was.

Chapter 15:

NIGHT FALLS

1334 BC, Regnal Year 17, Akhitaton (Modern Day Amarna)

In the seventeenth year of his reign, at the age of thirty-seven, Akhenaten was dead. Only the year before, he had elevated Nefertiti to co-regent where she began, almost immediately, to dismantle Akhenaten's religious reforms.

How did Akhenaten die? Did he fall victim to the plague like his mother and daughters? Did he die from complications from a congenital defect, the result of years of inbreeding among the royal family? Was it an accident? Was it murder?

He probably did not die of natural causes. He was still a relatively young man, much younger than his own father had been when he died. What is certain is that when Akhenaten died, his goals, his dreams, and his ideas died with him.

His tomb was not yet finished when he was laid to rest alongside his daughter, Meketaten. If Akhenaten's funeral differed from that of his predecessors, there is no record of it. In death, would the only son of the Aten employ the same rituals of his father? Or would his burial, like his life, be another radical departure from tradition? Did Nefertiti perform the Opening of the Mouth, or perhaps Smenkh-kare? And what of the little boy, Tutankhaten?

Jockeying for power and position among the elite began immediately after Akhenaten's death, as did a rejection of Atenism. For several years, through the brief reigns of Neferneferuaten and Smenkhare, the royal court remained at Akhitaton, but soon the residents abandoned this remote city, which had been built mainly to protect Akhenaten from his enemies. The tombs in the cliffs to the east went unfinished and unused. As the citizens returned to Thebes and Memphis, some of them believed that they might return some day. They boarded up their houses and carefully stored the belongings they couldn't take with them. Most never came back.

Neferneferuaten did not survive the year. No one knows what happened to her, and her mummy has never been found

Smenkhkare was gone within two years after that.

To lose three pharaohs in as many years indicates the depth of the political crisis facing Egypt. The infighting and treachery at court threatened to bring the entire nation down. Akhenaten consolidated power among his own hand-picked elite, and now they were at each other's throats, scrambling to create new alliances, and battling to see who would come out on top. With the sole member of the cult of Aten lying peacefully in his grave, there was a religious and political power vacuum that would need to be filled if Egypt was to survive.

One thing was clear: whatever shape the new regime took, it would need to mend fences. All three nexuses of power—the religious cults, the bureuacracy, and the military would have to come to some kind of agreement. The Amun priesthood, emboldened by the chaos, made demands of the remaining Atenist members of court. The city of Akhitaton must be abandoned and the capital returned to Thebes. Amun's temples must be restored and reopened and Amun himself returned to his rightful place at the top of the Egyptian pantheon. In return, the High Priests of Amun would throw their support behind the new pharaoh, whoever he was, and rally the Egyptian people to his side.

The military had some demands, too. The current head of the Egyptian military, a man named Horemheb, demanded a high position in the new government. Eventually, this ambitious man had himself named heir to the throne, in spite of the fact that he was not of royal blood, nor was he related to anyone in the royal family. In the interests of stability, the royal family agreed to name Horemheb Crown Prince, a title he would keep only until the new pharaoh had a son of his own.

But what were the demands of the remaining players who had supported Akhenaten? With three dead Atenist pharaohs, most of the loyalists at court were happy to make it out of Akhitaton alive. But at least two high-profile members of court required something in exchange for their cooperation with the military and the Amun priests.

The first was the High Priest of Aten, Meryra. As the highest religious official in what was still the most powerful cult, he held considerable sway during the transition. However, he knew the dangerous position he was in.

If the pharaohs weren't safe, then he was in even greater danger. In exchange for soothing over the resentment from the remaining Aten loyalists, Meryre asked only to return to Memphis permanently. When he got there, he changed his name back to its original Meryneith, blowing with the political winds like he had seventeen years prior.

The vizier Ay, the second Atenist to make his demands, was not so easily satisfied. Ay proved himself to be a true survivor. His life at court began as a faithful servant and brother-in-law to Amenhotep. From there he retained his power as Akhenaten's chief advisor, even after his sister Queen Tiye passed away. His friendships with the military and his long history at court allowed him to broker another deal, which insured the continuity of the Egyptian kingship and at the same time, cemented Ay's own position in the new regime. By this time, Ay was a very old man, but his political skill and shrewdness were perhaps the greatest story of the era.

Ay negotiated that the little boy, Tutankhaten, who was Akhenaten's only son, would become pharaoh, so as not to disrupt the line of succession. Ay himself would train, guide and manage Tut and act as an unofficial co-regent until the boy was of age and ready to take over the throne independently. Ay arranged a marriage between Tut and one of Nefertiti's daughters, just like the dead queen schemed from the moment Tut was born. Ay chose for Tut the youngest surviving girl, Ankhesenpaaten, who was about five years older than the prince. Tut grew to love her, trust her, and depend on her. In this way, Ay's control of the kingship through his female relatives continued from his sister Queen Tiye, to his daughter Nefertiti, to his grandaughter Ankhesenpaaten.

Eventually Ay would no longer be satisfied with "standing on the right side of the king." After decades of service to at least three different Pharaohs, Ay would become one himself and wear the Two Crowns of Upper and Lower Egypt.

As a gesture of good will and to send a clear message that a new era was dawning in Egypt, the religious capital was returned to Thebes, and the entire royal court departed Akhitaton for good. Finally, Tutankhaten, "Living Image of the Aten" and Ankhesenpaaten, "Living Through Aten," officially changed their names to reflect the healing of Egypt and a return to its traditional values.

She became Ankhesenamun, "Living through Amun".

He became Tutankhamun, "The Living Image of Amun".

The era of Atenism was over. Amun had won.

2010 AD, KV 55, Valley of the Kings, Luxor, Egypt

The process of examining the DNA of the mummy in KV55 took months. First, researchers working with Dr. Hawass inserted long needles into the bones of the mummy to retrieve its DNA. They had to keep the sample clear of any contaminating DNA from either themselves or from anyone in antiquity who had touched the body. After they pulled a sample, they sent it to the lab for the long process of preparing the sample for testing. Egyptian embalming methods ruined many DNA samples with the chemicals and resins used to preserve the body. Cleaning the samples of these foreign materials took weeks, and even if they managed to get a clean sample, DNA does not last forever. After thousands of years, it degrades, becoming increasingly difficult to work with.

Still, Dr. Hawass and his team managed to pull a usable sample from KV55, and they hoped it would reveal the identity of their mystery mummy. It did. The researchers had already identified several mummies from the 18th Dynasty, so they were able to match parents with children if a good sample was drawn. They knew the identity of Amenhotep, Akhenaten's father, so they first compared the KV55 mummy to him. The mummy tested positive as Amenhotep's son. However, Amenhotep had many wives and possibly many sons, so the next step was identifying the mother.

Because Queen Tiye's mummy had never been found, identifying the KV55 mummy as Tiye's son would take extra steps. Dr. Hawass sampled the mummies of Yuya and Tjuyu, known to be Queen Tiye's parents. From there, Hawass was able to find the formidable Queen Tiye herself. She was the mummy who had been known for years as only The Elder Lady. Her DNA tests revealed that she was indeed the mother of the mummy in KV55. But Tiye had at least two sons and possibly more. Some believed that Smenkhkare was not a son of Akhenaten but his brother, a much younger third son to Amenhotep and Tiye.

So the last step in solving the mystery was to determine the age of the mummy. This final step revealed the truth: the mummy was of a man who died between the ages of thirty-five and forty-five. Nothing is ever certain when studying ancient history, but Dr. Hawass and his researchers were confident that they had found Akhenaten.

The Amun priests curse was finally broken after three thousand years. Akhenaten — Heretic King, Evil One, Effective for the Aten — lived again.

EPILOGUE

50 Years After Akhenaten's Death

The Evil One would not live again.

Neither would his family nor any of his successors. The High Priests of Amun had seen to that.

Since Akhenaten's death, the Amun Priesthood had gone to great lengths to wipe the heretic's name from every statue, relief, and wall in Egypt. They accompanied the army to Akhitaton after it was abandoned and made sure the city was dismantled down to the ground. The *talatat* blocks, invented by Akhenaten to make construction in the city fast and efficient, proved equally easy to tear down. Horemheb used them as fill for his own construction projects. His workers took pleasure in turning the images of Nefertiti and Akhenaten upside down and crushing them under the weight of new temple walls. In places that could not be torn down, images of Akhenaten and Nefertiti were scratched out, smashed, hacked to pieces and painted over. During his reign, Akhenaten had issued a similar order to destroy Amun's idols and names. For the Amun priests, this vicious destruction of Akhenaten's name and image had been payback for all they suffered under the cult of the Aten.

The Amen priests taught the Egyptian people to hate and fear Akhenaten. They wiped him and his successors from every historical document. The great list of kings, which recorded each pharaoh's reign, skipped from Amenhotep III straight to Horemheb. It was as if Akhenaten, Neferneferuaten, Smenkhkare, Tutankhamun, and Ay never existed. The hundreds of clay Amarna tablets, a comprehensive historical record of the Aten government, were tossed aside, buried in the sand, and forgotten.

The Evil One would not live again.

After the abandonment of Akhitaton and the royal court's return to Thebes, Tut ordered that the mummies of his father, mother, and grandmother be retrieved from the Royal Wadi and buried closer to where Tut himself would be interred in the Kings Valley. Tut planned a grand tomb for himself that would be large enough to house his entire family, but it was not meant to be. Tut died young, before his twentieth birthday. He was childless, and with him the bloodline of the 18th Dynasty ended. Ay and Horemheb would be the last two pharaohs of this dynasty, but neither of them descended from the king.

The Amun priests spared only two mummies from Akhitaton, Queen Tiye and her daughter, who would later be known as the Younger Lady. She was a sister to Akhenaten, and three thousand years later, in 2010, Zahi Hawass would identify this Younger Lady as Tut's mother. The priests buried Tiye and her daughter together, and Queen Tiye avoided the stain of her son's legacy. Her role as Great Royal Wife to the most successful and revered pha-

raoh of all time, Amenhotep III, spared her the degrada-
tions visited on her son.

The Evil One would not live again.

This was the final step, the last ritual necessary to wipe
the memory of the heretic from history and condemn him to
death in the afterlife. As the priests of Amun descended into
the burial chamber, they did not buckle under the weight
of the coffin. It was a thrown together affair, originally
intended for a minor royal wife and adapted for the heretic.
It was not his original coffin, which had disappeared years
before the priests could retrieve it from Akhitaton. It contained no solid gold inner coffin, and the mummy inside
was already dried and broken in pieces.

When they finally reached the burial chamber, the priests
tossed the coffin carelessly onto a bier in a far corner. This
dark, empty crypt would be the heretic's final resting place.
No one could ever know the name of the Evil One, so one
of the priests hacked away Akhenaten's cartouches. In a
moment of fear or rage, another pulled half of the face off
of the lid. Another threw a rock, knocking the lid off kilter
and exposing the mummy to the air. The priests dumped
a few miscellaneous funerary items from the cursed city
of Akhitaton into a corner of the room. Anything of value
would eventually be stolen by tomb raiders anyway.

Under the dim light of their torches, the Amun priests
performed the final ritual, the final insult. They arranged the
Cardinal Blocks facing in toward the coffin. This king would

never escape his prison. No one would ever know who he was; his name would be forgotten, and Akhenaten himself would be wiped from the afterlife. The Amun priests smiled at their handiwork. They knew that for a man who cherished enlightenment, both literally and figuratively, there could be no worse fate than lying, forever alone, in a cold dark tomb cut off from the sun. The Amun priests had found the perfect punishment for Akhenaten's crimes.

The priests made their way up the long staircase and back into the fresh air of the Kings Valley. As they prepared to seal the door to the tomb, locking it forever, the High Priest of Amun stopped. He took his knife, and as a last act of victory and a malediction, scratched his curse into the wall.

The Evil One Shall Not Live Again.

ABOUT THE AUTHORS

Ramy Romany is a world-renowned Egyptologist, and has been has filming, producing, and being featured in documentaries and TV Shows for more than a decade.

Born into a documentary-producing family in Cairo, Egypt, Romany had the unique opportunity to hone his skillset from an early age while taking part in multiple active excavations and discoveries in Egypt. Romany's interest in Egyptology grew into an obsession and he became fascinated with studying the history, archaeology and language of his ancestors. This led him to purse a degree in Ancient Egyptian History and Archaeology from the University of Cairo. Romany can both read and write in Hieroglyphs.

Combining his passions of film and Egyptology, Romany was able to film, produce, direct and feature in over a hundred documentaries on Ancient Egypt for major international networks, all before the age of 20. An "Expert on all things Egyptian," as Joanna Lumley calls Romany on national British Television, Romany took Ewan McGregor into the great pyramids of Giza on *Long Way Down* for National Geographic. He was also the Egyptologist for *Ancient Aliens* on the History Channel for five seasons and was part of the team that discovered an underground pyramid using satellite imaging technology on the Discovery Channel's *Curiosity: Egypt: What Lies Beneath.*

After many years of filming documentaries on Ancient Egypt, political circumstances led Romany to flee his home in Egypt and relocate to Los Angeles, CA in 2011. This move provided a new network of contacts and opportunities to further showcase and expand his abilities. While Romany still resides in Los Angeles, CA with his wife and their three children, he continues to travel to locations across the globe filming, producing and being featured in documentaries and TV shows and takes at least one trip back to Egypt every year.

Emily Hache is a writer and story producer whose works include *Saving History: The Tomb of Tutankhamen* (for the Getty Conservation Institute), *Rudy Ruettiger: The Walk On, The Soul of Success: The Jack Canfield Story*, and *Armonia: Poverty into Life.* In 2016, she won a regional Emmy award for her work on the documentary, *Return to Esperanza*, about micro lending in the Dominican Republic. Previously she was a writer and development executive for the Walt Disney Company, DreamWorks SKG and Nickelodeon, where she developed the hit show *The Fairly*

OddParents. She traveled North America for two years in a twenty-three-foot motor home while filming *Found in America*, an adventure series she produced with her husband, cinematographer Rob Hache.

When she's not adventuring in exotic places, you can find her in Los Angeles, California with her husband and son and their poorly-behaved dog, Bandit.

For behind the scenes content and more visit

www.RamyRomany.com